# SNOW FLEAS TO SUNFLOWERS

## NOTES FROM THE NATURAL WORLD

Published by Friends of the University of Wisconsin - Madison Arboretum, Inc., 1207 Seminole Highway, Madison, Wisconsin 53711-3726.

Library of Congress Catalog Card Number: 97-61645
Hale, Jim.
Snow Fleas to Sunflowers

ISBN 0-9659523-0-4: $14.95

1. Education & Teaching   2. Gardening & Horticulture
3. Nature & Natural History


First Edition

# Snow Fleas to Sunflowers

## Notes from the Natural World

---

## Jim Hale

### Pat Brown, Editor

# CONTENTS

# ACKNOWLEDGMENTS

The publication of this book has been accomplished entirely by Friends of the Arboretum (FOA) volunteers who have donated their time and talents. All proceeds from its sale will go to the Friends of the Arboretum to support its programs.

In the spring of 1996, a core group of talented and energetic individuals who worked on *NewsLeaf*, the Friends of the Arboretum newsletter, formed the nucleus of this project — Bill Arthur, photographer; Linda Bishop, FOA volunteer program assistant; Pat Brown, editor; Virginia Kline, former Arboretum ecologist; Sara Minkoff, FOA volunteer coordinator; Dick Rehburg, FOA board member; and Paul Zukowski, writer.

Bill's talent for photography is evident on the cover of this book. Paul's marketing suggestions and proofreading skills have made this book a better product. Virginia's depth of scientific knowledge has contributed greatly to the accuracy of my articles. Dick's belief in this project helped convince the FOA Board to allocate funds for the book. Linda and Sara rounded up the volunteers who typed several years' worth of articles. Pat's desktop publishing and editorial experience took this book from an assortment of articles on computer disks to a printer-ready document — and her arm-twisting (in a nice way) resulted in Action Printing of Fond du Lac underwriting a part of the printing costs and Port-to-Print of Madison underwriting a portion of the electronic imaging expenses and assisting with the cover.

In addition to their individual talents, the group as whole served as trusted advisors, publishing and marketing consultants, and — most importantly — enthusiastic friends who share a love of the natural world and who wholeheartedly support restoration ecology in general and the Arboretum in particular.

Special thanks to *NewsLeaf* artists Patrick Shea and Elisabeth de Boor for the illustrations herein; to typists Joyce Carey, Maureen Conklin, Karen Delahaut, Jackie Finley, Olga Garca, Dorothy Haines and Carol Zimmerman; to proofreaders Bridget Brown, Jane Jacobs, and Nina Sossen; and graphic designer Sherry Donnino.

I am most indebted to former *NewsLeaf* editors who gave me so much good advice over the years — Barbara Atlee and Bonnie Hildebrand; to the Arboretum staff, including the late Gene Glover; to other artists who provided excellent sketches for my writings in *NewsLeaf* — Jane Bianco, Chuck Broehl and Jerry Morrow and to the past and present directors of the Friends of the Arboretum Board who found ways to finance this publication despite chronically limited budgets. And there is one more FOA member — my wife Pat. For more than 50 years she has encouraged and assisted my interests in the outdoors, for which I am everlastingly grateful.

Finally, I sincerely thank all those FOA members who took the trouble to tell me they liked what I wrote and encouraged an anthology. I'm amazed at how many of them there have been.

*Jim Hale*

# FOREWORD

Things seen and things happening outdoors at the University of Wisconsin-Madison Arboretum are the subject matter of this book. However, such natural events are not peculiar to one area. They can occur wherever native plants and animals are found in Wisconsin.

My writings about the outdoors that appear on the following pages had a long gestation period. It started in 1945 when I became both a graduate student at the University of Wisconsin in Madison and a two-year employee of the Arboretum as an assistant biologist. I learned much about the Arboretum's flora and fauna in this period. Next came a career as a professional wildlife biologist, followed by retirement, followed by an interest in volunteer work, all the while making visits to the Arboretum.

Then in 1988 I accepted an invitation to "do a little writing for *NewsLeaf*," the newsletter of the Friends of the Arboretum (FOA), the Arboretum's citizen-support organization.

One of my first assignments was a column about what was going on outdoors at the time. This quickly became a long-running monthly contribution. Finally, because of interest by FOA members, my columns were collected and recast into this book.

When these writings about the Arboretum first appeared in print they had the word "phenology" in their titles. We thought it was a neat way to alert readers about what would follow, but so many people asked the meaning of the term that we dropped it in favor of the more widely understood "outdoors."

However, phenology is still an important branch of biological science. It is the study of periodically recurring natural events, such as bird migration, plant flowering, freezing and thawing of lakes, insect emergence, and many others. Year-to-year records of these happenings are not only interesting as they occur, but also help us understand the inner workings of the land.

Phenological data has been recorded for years by a wide variety of biological scientists — agronomists, meteorologists, botanists, entomologists, foresters and ornithologists, to name a few. Aldo Leopold wrote of phenology that "whoever sees the land as a whole is likely to have an interest in it." A 3,000-year-old phenology can be found in the Old Testament:

> *"For lo, the winter is past, the rain is over and gone. The flowers appear on the earth, and the voice of the turtledove is heard in our land."*
>
> Song of Solomon 2:11-12

SPRING

# PHENOLOGY

March is a month of contrasts. The weather can bring balmy days or blizzards, sunshine or showers. The sun is higher and the days are longer, so snow and cold are easier to take.

The pace of nature again is picking up. As bird migrations begin, I like to look for four species that to me have become true harbingers of spring: the first skein of northward-bound Canada geese riding a southerly wind, an American woodcock sky-dancing in the Arboretum's dusk, the loud cries of a killdeer winging overhead, and the musical call of an eastern bluebird perched on a crab tree in the Longenecker Gardens.

There is a mystery or two in March. Take the American robin singing from a treetop at the McKay Center. Is he a new arrival from the south, or is he a resident that spent the winter around the Wingra Springs? No one really knows.

More bird songs can be heard. Our resident mourning doves and northern cardinals have been calling for several weeks. Starlings and common grackles wheeze and creak in what passes for their spring song. Meadowlarks are in full song. Great blue herons add an occasional squawk.

New migrants can be seen almost daily. Tundra swans, American coots, and ducks such as lesser scaup and common goldeneyes might be spotted in patches of open water as the ice melts on our lakes. Fox sparrows in brushy woods edges, horned larks on rural roadsides, sandhill cranes overhead and northern harriers coursing open fields are all a part of March. More sounds come from chorus and cricket frogs as marsh edges thaw.

American crows can be seen carrying nesting materials. If you're lucky enough to find a great horned owl nest, it's likely the adult owls will be feeding good-sized young; they're very early nesters.

Hibernating mammals are beginning to emerge. Look for eastern chipmunks and woodchucks out and about on sunny days. Little brown bats are flying at dusk.

Warm spells also bring many insects out of hiding places. Mourning cloak and red admiral butterflies are especially attractive. Honey bees are investigating the blossoms of maple trees. At the Wingra Springs, look for half-inch-long, dark stone flies creeping about on the rocks. They belong to a group of insects that emerge in late winter while snow still lies on the ground and are collectively known as "snow insects."

Springtails (or snow fleas) are minute, black insects that swarm on the surface of the snow on the sunny side of trees during warm days. Several species of midges (*Diptera*) may appear in aerial swarms over spring waters. Fortunately for us, the biting mosquitos and black flies won't come until later.

Plants are starting to stir, too. The most obvious are the skunk cabbages around Skunk Cabbage Bridge at the east end of Wingra Woods, and the "pussywillow" stage of catkins on the brushy willows in wetlands. Yellow and red flowers of the silver (or soft) maple trees appear. Red-osier dogwood stems turn brilliant red, justifying their name. Hazel catkins are expanding. Hard (sugar) maple and box elder sap is running.

You may not think of red as a spring color, but a male northern cardinal in full breeding plumage perched at the top of a brightly colored red-osier dogwood along the edge of West Marsh is a spring sight long to remember.

April can be more interesting, if instead of merely watching the new spring develop its ever-wonderful bird migrations and early wildflowers, you try adding a new dimension — sound.

Many of April's birds can be identified by their calls and don't have to be seen. Sit quietly on the open slope south of the Wingra Woods parking lot and listen. A sunny and windless day is the best.

You might hear the loud "wick-wick-wick-wick" call of a common flicker from the edge of the woods. Or the double-noted squawk of a ring-necked pheasant rooster. Or the noisy "kill-dee" call of a passing killdeer. Or the musical two-note call of an eastern bluebird.

Cawing American crows or honking Canada geese overhead are sometimes heard but not seen. Courting flights of mallards can include the strident quacking of the hen and the quiet "yeeb" notes of her suitors in the chase.

Later, at dusk, the song flights and nasal "peent" notes of American woodcock, and the winnowing "hoohoohoohoo" display flight of common snipe are April specialties. At night, if the air is calm, flocks of migrating small songbirds can be heard constantly sounding their faint cheeps and peeps as they pass.

April sounds aren't all avian. Chipmunks chirping are easy to recognize, but often confused with bird calls. It's the breeding season for frogs, so the distinctive calls of many species such as chorus frogs and spring peepers can be heard near or in wetlands.

When April brings you outdoors, stop, look *and* listen.


May is the birdwatcher's month, a time when the variety of birds you can find in the state reaches its annual peak in a great array of migrant and resident birds.

It's a time for the wood warblers — small, colorful, hyperactive singers of which more than 30 species live in or pass through

Wisconsin. At least four species nest in the Arboretum — yellow warbler, common yellowthroat, ovenbird, and American redstart.

Other natural events of May are less obvious. Franklin's ground squirrels finally emerge from hibernation. The young of small mammals should be appearing, especially cottontail rabbits. First fawns of white-tailed deer also are born this month.

Many late-spring wildflowers will come into first bloom in May. On Greene Prairie, look for lupine, golden alexanders, shooting star, puccoon, phlox and yellow lady's-slipper. In the woods or at woods edges you should find jack-in-the-pulpit, wild crab, blackberry, white trillium, mayapple, black cherry, and many others.

Don't forget that May means wild asparagus and morel mushrooms — and don't neglect to consult carefully a good guide before sampling the latter. And finally, be prepared to cope with mosquitoes and deer flies while you're outdoors.

How lucky we are that these spring events can be seen without fee or cover charge. How lucky we are that this new season occurs each year in spite of us and not because of us. Enjoy what can be seen, and pity those who do not care to enjoy them with you.

Cherish the spring. For bright sun, snow-melt and bird song. For warm wind, soft rain and new green. For bare head, shed coat and wet shoes. Spring is joy.

# Plants, Animals & Other Things in Season

## Secret Sources

Wildflowers are one of the most delightful things about spring. Did you ever wonder how they can appear so quickly after snowmelt? Their secret is in their roots, which we seldom see, but which are the source of their strength and beauty.

Most early spring flowers grow from fleshy underground rootstocks which may be large and many years old. They are the heart and soul of the plant, spending the growing season in providing nutrients for flowering, leaf growth, seed set, and most importantly, storing nourishment for immediate growth when spring comes again.

Wildflower roots come in many shapes and sizes. Some species have rounded tubers, some have long rhizomes, some grow laterally just under the soil surface, and some grow directly down to depths of several feet. Perennial plants can survive without flowers and leaves, but not without roots.

Over the centuries, wild roots have had many uses seldom seen today, especially as food and medicine. The early spring roots of trout lilies (*Erythronium*), for example, are edible when raw, but are said to grow sweeter if they are dried first. Toothwort (*Dentaria*) has a sharp taste suitable for food seasoning and was widely used as a remedy for toothaches.

Roots of dandelions (*Taraxacum*), a weed not native to Wisconsin, have been roasted and ground as a substitute for coffee and as an ingredient of homemade beer. A dandelion-root elixir was once favored as a spring tonic, a use recorded by Arabs as long ago as the 10th century.

Many of our spring flowers have poisonous roots, but nevertheless have been favored as medicine by American Indians. Pasque flower (*Anemone*) roots were used in treating snake bites. Yellow lady's-slippers (*Cypripedium*) provided a nerve stimulant and antispasmodic.

Mayapple (*Podophyllum*) is unusual in that its roots and leaves are poisonous, but its *ripe* fruit is not (unripe fruits are poisonous). Its roots provide a violent purgative and are still used in commercial "liver pills." Jack-in-the-pulpit (*Arisaema*) roots, also poisonous, when dried and ground were said to cure headaches if sprinkled on the scalp.

Bloodroot (*Sanguinaria*) and puccoon (*Lithospermum*) have roots filled with red juices used by Indians for body paint and dying furs, baskets and other decorations.

There's more to May wildflowers than meets the eye.


## FOUR FAVORITE FIRSTS

As the world awakens after a long, hard winter, April becomes a month for plant watchers. The annual round of new growth and flowering has begun, so now there is a question: When is spring really here?

The answer varies with the individual. For some, it might be when the first bluebird arrives, or when Lake Wingra is ice-free, or when the first redwing sings from a cattail stalk, or when the maple sap is running.

For me, however, I know spring truly has arrived when I can find my four favorite flowers in bloom at the Arboretum. They are the pasque flower, hepatica, dutchman's breeches and bloodroot. All four are among the very earliest to appear, the pasque flower on the Grady Knolls or Pasque Flower Hill, and the others in Gallistel or Wingra Woods. If you'd like to raise my list of favorite firsts to 10, add toothwort, wood anemone, spring beauty and bellwort in the woods, plus puccoon and birdfoot violet on the prairies.

Pasque flowers usually bloom first, sometimes as early as March. The whole plant is covered with long silky hairs. The flower stalk seems to sprout from a clump of silvery hair, and leaves may not appear until flowering is completed. The feathery seed heads are conspicuous in late spring. The pasque flower was one of the first wildflowers I was taught to recognize by my grandmother. Before I was a teenager, it was an annual event to go with grandma to find pasque flowers (she called them "windflowers") along a railroad right-of-way south of town.

Hepaticas are usually the earliest flowers in the woods. They grow only a few inches tall and their flowers may be white, blue, pink or lavender. Their three-lobed leaves have given rise to another name — liverleaf — because of their shape. There are two species, both having similar habitats, found in Wisconsin. One has rounded leaf lobes; the other's lobes are pointed.

The white flowers of dutchman's breeches grow several to a stalk and appear like pantaloons hung up to dry. You have to look at them upside down to get the full effect, since the "breeches" hang waist down and legs up. This plant has delicately dissected pale green leaves and is a relative of the home gardener's bleeding heart.

The flower bud of bloodroot grows wrapped in a single rounded leaf which expands after the two-inch white flower opens. Bloodroot gets its name from the red color of the rootstalk from which one flower grows in spring. Its red juice was used by many Native Americans for body paint, dyeing furs and baskets, and painting other objects. The men of the Omaha tribe believed the red juice to be a love charm: a red spot applied with a fingertip to a girl's cheek made her his forever.

## SKUNK CABBAGE — THE SMELL OF SPRING

If you're looking for signs of spring in the plant world, the good news is that skunk cabbage (*Symplocarpus foetidus*) will be in flower by early March. In fact, its annual growth usually begins in February.

Both leaves and flowers grow from stout rootstalks. The unusual flower parts come up before the leaves. A four-to-eight-inch mottled purple, brown and green hood-like structure called a spathe appears first. Within the spathe grows a nearly spherical fleshy stem called a spadix, which becomes crowded with small, thick-sepaled flowers. After pollination, the spathe dies back and fruit is formed from the whole mass of flowers. Leaves sprout in tightly rolled cones which expand to be about three feet long and a foot wide.

Skunk cabbage is a wet-soil plant partial to swampy ground, usually near water. Its showplace in the Arboretum is at Skunk Cabbage Bridge near the east end of Wingra Woods. Skunk cabbage is a close relative of our familiar wild jack-in-the-pulpit and the well-known house plant, *Dieffenbachia*.

The bad news is that skunk cabbage smells awful and tastes worse. All parts of the plant have a pronounced skunk-like odor, especially when broken. The odor, however, helps the plant by attracting carrion flies and other pollinating insects to its blossoms.

Another unusual characteristic is that the growing spathe can produce enough metabolic heat to melt the February snows through which it sprouts. The heat protects the plant from freezing and volatilizes its own odor to make the flowers more attractive to pollinators. The spathe also produces a warm haven for the visiting insects.

Don't try to eat skunk cabbage. Cooking does not remove the bad taste. Also, the entire plant is full of needle-sharp crystals of calcium oxalate that will imbed themselves in your mouth, causing violent burning sensations and soreness lasting for hours. In extreme cases, the crystals cause swelling of the tongue and throat which can block breathing.

Medicinal uses of skunk cabbage by Native Americans are said to include a decoction from dried roots taken to treat venereal diseases. However, this drink taken three times daily for three weeks was reputed to make the drinker sterile. Some tribes were said to use the odor of crushed leaves as a treatment for headaches. This sounds like a case of the cure being worse than the disease.

## THE POTATO CHIP TREE

In the Arboretum's oak woods you can find trees with bark that looks like a popular snack. They are called "potato chip trees." Its true name is black cherry (*Prunus serotina*), but it gained a nickname because of its scaly bark that peels off in flakes like potato chips. The bark makes this tree easy to identify, even without leaves or fruit.

Black cherries are native in all our eastern states from Maine to Florida and west to the prairies. It's a medium-sized forest tree growing to 60 or more feet in height and three feet in diameter. The other Wisconsin wild cherries (choke, pin and sand) are close relatives that are smaller trees or shrubs.

Drooping clusters of white flowers appear in May as the leaves are starting to grow, and the pea-sized ripe fruits that follow the flowers are dark purple. The Latin specific name (*serotina*) means "appearing late" as a comparison to domestic cherries which produce flowers before leaves.

Black cherry twigs and bark contain prussic acid and when crushed have an almond aroma and sweet taste. However, mature plant parts (except the fruit) can become poisonous. Wilted leaves, for example, are especially dangerous to livestock.

The fruit, roots and bark of black cherry are used to produce an extract long popular in old-fashioned home remedies and doctors' prescriptions. J.E. Rogers wrote that "no spring tonic is seriously expected to rid us of 'that tired feeling' unless the tang of wild cherry is there." Pioneers simply chewed the leaf buds in spring "to purify the blood" and to save on doctor bills at the same time.

The wood of black cherry is excellent for furniture and ranks close to black walnut for this purpose.

Wild cherries are a very important wildlife food. Deer and rabbits browse the twigs and bark. Mice and chipmunks eat the fruit as do many songbirds such as robins, starlings and cedar waxwings. It isn't unusual to see small flocks of birds feeding in a single tree when fruit is ripening. Many black cherry trees get their start after passing through the digestive tract of a bird.

## A Friendly Spring Weed

Thoughts of spring wildflowers usually center on such favorites as hepatica, bloodroot, or pasque flower. They certainly never dwell on one of the most common, unassuming, early-flowering plants — shepherd's purse.

A member of the Mustard family, it grows wherever it finds a patch of disturbed ground, in any kind of soil, worldwide. Recently a friend encountered it high in a remote desert canyon of Utah. The wiry stem may be from two to 36 inches tall, with small, variably-shaped leaves, usually including a rosette at the base.

The four-petalled flowers are always clustered toward the top of the stem. The seed pods lining the main stalk on short stems are flat and heart-shaped. They are the plant's most obvious characteristic and provide its Latin name, *Capsella bursa-pastoris*, roughly translated as "little capsule that is the purse of the shepherd."

Each plant of this abundant and persistent species produces thousands of seeds that are spread by the wind. Those that sprout in fall will overwinter as leafy basal rosettes and begin their growth and flowering in spring as soon as the ground thaws. Therefore, the plant can be found in bloom from April to the fall freeze.

Introduced from Europe, the plant is considered a weed here. Nevertheless, it has value. It can be used as a salad green. It is classed as a medicinal plant; herbalists use it for stopping internal hemorrhage. Of more modern importance is its place in genetic research; this plant was used to develop the principles used in corn hybridization.

It is one of those plants which remind us, in this time of biological extinctions, that even the most lowly or unregarded life forms have both a potential value to us and an intrinsic importance in the scheme of nature.

## THE FUNGUS AMONG US

Wild mushrooms mean different things to different people. Some of us love to eat them; others are afraid to try for fear of being poisoned. Some of us think they're beautiful in form and color; others call them ugly and disgusting.

Many of us call the edible kinds "mushrooms" and the poisonous kinds "toadstools," but this distinction has no scientific basis. If anything, it's an insult to the toads, who have nothing to do with mushrooms. Whether you're for or against them, mushrooms are a most interesting part of the plant world.

Mushrooms are fungi and are relatives of such other fungi as the mildew on cloth, mold on bread, or rusts that blight grain fields. Many fungi grow in dark and damp locations, but mushrooms in their most attractive forms grow in woods and grassy fields where many varieties appear in the spring. Mushrooms do not manufacture their own food and therefore must grow on organic matter which can supply them with nutrients, such as decaying wood (although some grow in association with living tree roots), rotted leaf litter and standing dead trees.

The mushroom we see is only part of a whole fungus. The main part of the plant is hidden in the ground and is composed of long, tangled threads of cells called a mycelium. A mycelium may live for many years and grow to cover many square feet.

The above-ground mushroom is the fungus' equivalent of a fruit. It is short-lived and grows from its mycelium for the purpose of reproduction, just as do the flowering stems of the higher plants. However, mushrooms do not have seeds. Instead, each mushroom produces literally millions of dust-like spores on the underside of its cap. These minute structures become windblown, and if they fall on a favorable spot will germinate. Very few spores reach this stage.

Mushrooms have been eaten for centuries. The ancient Greek and Roman epicures held them in high esteem. A great deal of experimenting has been done to determine which species are edible and which are poisonous. Even today, the edibility of a few species remains uncertain. All of this points up the need to know which mushroom is which. Mistakes can be fatal.

If you are a mushroom hunter, or want to become one, there are two important rules to follow. First, don't try to identify all the mushrooms. With the help of knowledgeable experts, and any of several good field guides, learn how to identify four or five of the most edible kinds and ignore the rest. Second, and this is the Golden Rule, if you are not absolutely sure what species you have, DO NOT EAT IT.

Botanist C.M. Christiansen has identified a group of mushrooms as "The Foolproof Four." They are all common, easily identified, edible and choice. They are the morel (*Morchella*), puffball (*Calvatia*), shaggy mane (*Coprinus*), and sulfur polypore (*Polyporus*).

The morel (sometimes called sponge mushroom because of its appearance) has a pointed and pitted cap with convoluted ridges. It grows to a height of about four inches in spring. It is found in the oak woods of southern Wisconsin and in the maple forests of the north. Locations of productive morel sites are jealously guarded by most mushroom hunters.

Puffballs are roughly spherical in shape and range in size from smaller than a golf ball to a foot in diameter. They are white in color and should be picked while they are still firm and completely white inside and out when split, and do not have any dark colors or worm holes. They occur throughout the growing season.

Shaggy manes have elongated caps with a scaly-looking (though soft) surface and grow four to six inches tall. They are one of the inky-cap group, so named because as they age, the edges of their caps turn black and melt into a black liquid. Avoid picking them at this stage; they're not poisonous, but they don't taste good.

The sulfur polypores (or sulfur shelf mushrooms) form massive orange and yellow rosettes of overlapping, fan-shaped leaves. They grow most often on dead oak wood. Fall is the best time to find them. The younger stages make the best eating.

If you want to add more species to your preferred list, two common and easily identified ones are honey caps (*Armillaria*) and meadow mushrooms (*Agaricus*). The latter genus includes the forerunners of the species now commonly cultivated for produce markets.

Freshly picked mushrooms (the edible ones, of course) taste best when fried in butter or stewed. They can be served as a side dish, added to casseroles and omelets, or as a topping for steaks, roasts or toast. Mushrooms can also be dried in the sun or in an oven for future use.

As your knowledge of mushrooms increases, you will find that much folklore exists about them. For example, the old Romans said don't pick mushrooms that grow near a serpent's hole or a rusty nail because they will be poisonous. The fairy-ring mushroom grows in circles several feet in diameter on lawns and golf courses; such a growth pattern was said to define a dancing ground of fairies, or to be caused by a lightning strike.

A ripe puffball shoots clouds of its spores out a hole in its top when given a bump; hence its name. Its spores have been used in the past as a styptic powder to stop bleeding, and were once believed to cause permanent blindness if you got them in your eyes (which we now know is not true).

Always remember that the odds are not in your favor when you collect unidentified mushrooms for the table. If you're not absolutely sure what it is, just say "no."

# LUPINE BLUE

When the next soft, warm morning comes along in late May, take an early walk into the Arboretum's Greene Prairie. As the sun rises over the oaks to the east, enjoy the bluish haze engulfing the north side of the prairie. You'll be taking in the annual display of the lupines.

Wild lupine (*Lupinus perennis*) is a major player in our cast of spring prairie flowers. It is partial to open areas with dry, sandy, infertile soils from Minnesota to Maine and south to Missouri and Florida. In Wisconsin, it is often an indicator of a remnant sand prairie.

Lupine plants are easy to identify, growing one to two feet tall with showy spikes usually of blue, but sometimes pink or white, flowers. Lupines are members of the bean family (*Fabaceae*). Their leaves are palmate, with seven to 11 leaflets. By July, the flowers will have matured into round seeds contained in pods.

The lupine genus is widely distributed in temperate zones, with several hundred species worldwide. Taxonomists consider their identification to be difficult. Fortunately, the Midwest has only one major species — the one that grows in Greene Prairie. Another lupine species is the small bluebonnet of which Texas is so proud.

Cultivated lupines favored by home gardeners are mostly aliens from Europe and Asia. Our native wild lupine can be grown from seed and transplanted to suitable sites, but garden guides note that mature plants have deep woody roots and it is a waste of time to try to transplant them.

The name of the plant is derived from the Latin word for wolf (*lupus*), based on an early belief, now known to be false, that lupine roots robbed the soil of its nutrients.

Wild lupine plays a part in current endangered species programs. Both Wisconsin and the U.S. Fish and Wildlife Service list the Karner blue butterfly (*Lycaeides*) as an endangered species. Lupine comes into the picture because it is the major host plant for the Karner blue. This butterfly is seldom, if ever, found where wild lupine is absent. Its current range is primarily those parts of the oak and pine barrens in central and northwestern Wisconsin where wild lupine occurs.

## SEX AND THE SINGLE CATKIN

After a long winter and a cold early spring, it's nice to see all the spring blooms returning. We welcome hepatica, bloodroot, trout lily and trillium as old friends. But it's surprising how many spring wildflowers we seldom notice.

For a change of pace, take a longer look at the trees and shrubs around you. Some trees and shrubs, including cherry, apple and wild plum, have flowers with conspicuous petals that attract insect pollinators.

In some, including hazelnut and several species of trees, small, inconspicuous, wind-pollinated flowers are packed closely together in catkins. These won't make a bouquet, but their end product is the same as any other flower — a new generation.

Some catkins, such as those of the birch family, can be seen in winter when they are small and stiff. In spring they become long and flexible. Some catkins remain hidden in buds until the buds open in spring. Pussy willows are a good example.

Their "pussies" are immature catkins. Catkins may be "imperfect," producing only male stamens (which make pollen) or female pistils (which produce fruit), or they may be "perfect" because each flower has both stamens and pistils.

From here on the sex business gets complicated. It varies greatly from one tree family to another. The willow family's catkins are usually all male or all female, generally with only one type on a tree. Cottonwoods are a good example; nobody seems to like a female cottonwood when its fuzzy seeds are blowing all over the neighborhood. In the oak family, flowers of both sexes appear on the same tree, but only the male flowers are borne in catkins.

The birch family has male and female catkins on the same tree. The female catkin is small and erect, while the male catkin is elongated and drooping. A good example of the family is the red or river birch (*Betula nigra*) that grows on the front lawn of the McKay Center. Its bark is reddish in color compared to the more common white birch, but its catkins are definitely typical of the birch family.

River birch is a Wisconsin native found along major waterways in the southwest quarter of the state. We are at the northwest corner of its continental range.

The maple family is diverse; some species have flowers of only one sex per tree, while others may have both sexes in the same flower. The elm family has perfect flowers.

So when you're out flower-watching this spring, if you look up as well as down you won't miss some interesting blossoms.

# HERE TODAY, GONE TOMORROW

The early spring wildflowers in Gallistel and Wingra Woods have similar but different growth habits that fall into two groups. Both areas include plants that bloom, put on annual growth and produce seeds in the short time between snow-melt and the leafing-out of trees.

One group, known as "spring ephemerals," includes dutchman's breeches, spring beauty, trout lily and toothwort. They are the plants that die back for the year after they become shaded by tree leaf growth.

The second group, however, retain their leaves into the summer and become shade plants for the rest of the year. Bloodroot, hepatica, Jack-in-the-pulpit, and mayapple are examples.

One of the lesser-known species in the second group is twinleaf (*Jeffersonia diaphylla*), an uncommon resident of Wisconsin's southern counties, including the Arboretum's Gallistel Woods. Its continental range extends from Ontario to Wisconsin and south to Alabama. It is a member of the Barberry family, which also includes a couple of other Arboretum favorites — blue cohosh and mayapple.

Twinleaf has several unusual characteristics. Its leaves, borne one to a 10-inch stalk, are so deeply cleft that they resemble butterfly wings when viewed from above. Although the name "twinleaf" implies two leaves per stem, there really is only one odd-shaped leaf.

The flowers are white, flat, about an inch in diameter, have eight petals, and grow singly on a leafless stem. They have a very short blooming time, often lasting less than a day.

Twinleaf seeds grow in a fleshy capsule that has a hinged lid at the top. Seeds are believed to be spread in part by ants that carry the seeds to their nests where they eat the remaining fleshy parts but leave the seeds.

The Gallistel Woods twinleaf population occurs in several large clumps resulting from transplanting done many years ago. The plants are attractive and seem to grow well in any moist, shady spot, but their abbreviated blooming period makes them less desirable for gardens.

If you find a twinleaf flower today, don't expect to see it again tomorrow.

# A Spring Caller

I'm looking forward to one of those warm, sunny, March days when the snow is nearly gone and a soft breeze is in the south. Such is the time when the first robins, bluebirds, redwings and grackles are returning. But there is one more bird on the wing whose call says to me "Spring is really here," and that is the killdeer.

Its familiar "kill-dee, kill-dee" call overhead while I'm hiking the edges of the Arboretum prairies is a welcome forecast of warmer weather to come.

Killdeers are robin-sized shorebirds and are one of the plover group. The two black bands on their white chests, plus a red-brown rump and tail feathers, are characteristics found on no other shorebird.

They frequent short-grass meadows, plowed farm fields, shores, golf courses, riverbanks and graveled roadsides. Occasionally one will turn up around a spring hole in midwinter, but most killdeers spend the cold months in the southern United States and Mexico.

A killdeer's diet is almost exclusively insects, worms, grubs and other invertebrates, with a few weed seeds thrown in now and then. They don't build nests in the traditional sense, but simply lay a clutch of four eggs in a slight hollow in an open area with short grass or stony bare ground. A few pebbles or twigs may be added, but otherwise the eggs are exposed.

Chicks leave the nest as soon as their natal down dries and follow their parents about immediately thereafter. The downy chicks' coloring is so similar to the adults that there is no mistaking their identity.

One of the killdeer's most engaging habits is its distraction display. A pair with a nest or brood make valiant attempts to lure away predators by flying about with loud calls, then dropping to the ground near the intruder and limping away with tails spread, one wing in the air and the other flailing the ground as they attempt to prevent discovery of their eggs or young.

If a displaying bird succeeds in leading the intruder away for up to several hundred feet, it will suddenly drop its broken-wing act and take flight back to the area where the whole performance started — remarkable behavior indeed.

Killdeers were named for their calls. Their specific Latin name is "*vociferus.*" Their common name is obviously a phonetic translation, but why an "r" was added when "kill-dee" is more accurate is uncertain.

## Leaf Dancers

While you're out some warm April afternoon looking for the first hepatica and bloodroot blooms, you may be startled, especially if the winds are calm, to see and hear dead leaves dancing on the ground. Often the leaping leaves may hide their cause. What you've probably found is one of three spring birds that are most proficient at rummaging in the dried vegetation under thickets and at woods edges.

Perhaps the champion noisemaker is the rufous-sided towhee. This long-tailed, black-and-white songbird with brick-red sides (females are brown where males are black) is slightly smaller than a robin and spends much time on the ground. It scratches vigorously with both feet and tosses leaves to the side with its bill in its search for something to eat. The towhee is better known for its song, a loud "drink-your-teeee," than it is for its feeding habits.

A smaller leaf-tosser is the fox sparrow, a heavily striped, red-brown skulker in the brush. It also attacks dead leaves with great enthusiasm and can cause considerable commotion in the process. Its song has been characterized as "loud, rich, brilliant and musical." This means that field-guide authors haven't found a good translation into English words as they have for the simpler song of the towhee.

The third member of the trio is the brown thrasher. This robin-sized bird has a curved bill, long tail, red-brown back and striped undersides. It probably is the champion when it comes to long-distance leaf-throwing, but it is not as powerful a scratcher as the fox sparrow or towhee. The thrasher, too, has a loud and melodious song that is usually performed in couplets while perched well up in a tree.

Occasionally other birds can be found in the spring leaf-moving derby. Bluejays will indulge, often in a search for left-over acorns as well as insects. Common grackles also do it, but they operate mostly as tossers and not scratchers. Even a late-migrant dark-eyed junco is sometimes seen scratching up a meal among the leaves.

## A FRIENDLY FLYCATCHER

About 60 years ago, when my grandmother was teaching me which bird was which, the phoebe became one of my early spring favorites.

This bird, known properly as the eastern phoebe, comes to Wisconsin in late March, and its northward migration continues through April. The timing of its movement is geared to the first warm days of spring that bring out new hatches of the insects on which it feeds.

Phoebes are sparrow-sized, dark brownish-gray birds without prominent markings. They do, however, have two easily noted characteristics. The first is their song, a repeated rendition of their name, a raspy and emphatic "fee-bee," or perhaps more accurately "wheepy," that is sharply accented on the first syllable. Their second trait is a frequent bobbing of their tails.

Phoebes are in the flycatcher family, and like other fly-catchers, insects compose about 90 percent of their diet, with the remainder made up of small berries and seeds. They hunt by making frequent short sallies in pursuit of insects from perches on trees, fence posts or utility wires, returning to their perch after each flight to keep watch for another meal.

One reason I like phoebes is that they are people-friendly. Almost any rural home, shed, or barn might house a pair of phoebes nesting under low-hanging eaves. Their nests are tidy creations of soft grasses covered with bits of moss.

Writing in 1942, Winson M. Tyler summed up the phoebe this way: "The phoebe is a gentle little bird, dull in plumage with scarcely a field mark. He is light and easy on the wing, making swift, adroit turns and twists and sudden tumblings ... and when he lights airily on his perch, his tail keeps swaying loosely, almost as if blown by the wind.

"He and his mate may settle in a busy, noisy farmyard, or perhaps far away in a remote rocky glen, but wherever they nest they will spend a peaceful summer, giving little heed to their neighbors, seemingly happy, contented and self-sufficient, devoting themselves to the care of their family."

## SPIRIT OF THE MARSHES

Let's set an April scene with a quote from ornithologist A. C. Bent: "On the wings of the south wind comes the first wisp of snipe, the will-o-the wisp of the marshes, here today and gone tomorrow, coming and going under the cover of darkness. All through the spring migration, ... we may hear the weird, winnowing sound of the snipe's courtship flight, a tremulous humming, loud and penetrating, audible at a long distance. One is both thrilled and puzzled when he hears it for the first time, for it seems like a disembodied sound, the sighing of some wandering spirit, ... a rapidly pulsating 'who-who-who-who-who-who-who-who,' increasing and then decreasing again in intensity."

The source of this unusual sound is a cousin of the American woodcock and the other shorebirds, the common snipe (*Gallinago gallinago*). This species was formerly known to birdwatchers as the Wilson snipe, and is still called jacksnipe by most hunters.

Snipe are chunky, patterned brown and white, long-billed, short-legged waders slightly smaller than a woodcock. In Wisconsin, they are considered fairly common summer residents, with a nesting range mostly in the central and northern sections of the state. During their spring migration, they favor any low, open land: sedge marshes with scattered shrubs; mud flats and stream banks.

Snipe can often be heard in the Arboretum at dusk, about the same time that woodcock begin their evening song flights. The snipe's ghostly winnowing is not a vocalization, but is produced by wing and tail feathers. The bird rises high into the air and flies an erratic, swooping course. In each dive, the tail feathers are spread and the wings are partly closed. The tail feathers vibrate with a humming noise. This vibration is slightly interrupted by air flow through the wings, producing the tremulous sound which we call winnowing. These winnowing flights are part of a breeding-season ritual and may take place at any hour, but most often in early evening.

Common snipe were extremely abundant in the late 1800s, but over-shooting drastically reduced their numbers. Since the institution of hunting controls in the early 1900s, snipe populations have recovered to a seemingly safe level, but their former abundance has not been reached and probably never will be. However, there are plenty of snipe to provide the remarkable winnowing that so enhances our April evenings.

# A Small Mammal with a Big Attitude

As the melting snow uncovers your back yard, you may see a network of inch-wide trails meandering across the grass. If you follow their wandering, crooked lines they probably will lead you to a burrow under a pile of old leaves, into your garden, under your back steps or to some other hiding place. These trails are nearly always made by shrews, which are small mammals that look like mice but aren't.

Shrews have a family of their own (Soricidae), and are more closely related to moles than to mice. The most common species in our area are the short-tailed shrew *(Blarina)* and the long-tailed shrew *(Sorex)*, both of which have small eyes and ears, pointed snouts, dark gray or black fur, and are four to five inches long, including their tails.

A third, more scarce species found in the Madison area is the pigmy shrew *(Microsorex)*. At three and one-half inches long, it's the smallest mammal found in Wisconsin.

Except during mating periods, shrews seem to be solitary, although they get together often enough to rear two litters per summer, which average about seven young each.

Shrews are most active at night, but often hunt food during the day as well, due to the remarkable demands of their high metabolic rates. Captive shrews have been known to eat up to two times their weight per day. They do not hibernate and they are in constant motion year-round, unless they are asleep, which is not often.

Shrews feed on insects, earthworms, snails and other small invertebrates. They are also predators of baby mice and nestling birds when they can find them.

Shrews have unpleasant personalities. Mammalogist H.H.T. Jackson wrote that a shrew is "an active, vicious, highstrung, and restless little imp." He later added "nervous and irritable" to his characterization. They fight savagely with any of their own kind not their mate and will attempt to kill any other small creature they come across. We should be glad shrews aren't Wisconsin's largest mammals.


# A Graceful Glider

The Arboretum is home to one of Wisconsin's prettiest mammals, the southern flying squirrel *(Glaucomys volans)*. This little squirrel is the smallest of our tree squirrels, being about half the size of its well-known cousin, the gray squirrel.

Flying squirrels have soft, dense fur that is uniformly gray-brown on their upper sides and pure white below. Their ears and eyes are large, providing a pleasing appearance.

Flying squirrels claim mature oak or maple woodlands as their home. They also regularly take up residence in attics and farm outbuildings close to wooded areas. They are almost entirely nocturnal and hence are not often seen by non-nocturnal humans. It is not always easy to detect their presence in a given area — unless they are scurrying around your attic in the middle of the night.

In wooded areas, they occupy tree cavities such as old woodpecker nest sites. Several squirrels may occupy the same nest, especially in winter. If you spot such possible nest holes, beating sharply on the trunk of the tree with a stout stick sometimes will cause a squirrel to peek out and possibly emerge completely to see what's going on.

Flying squirrels do not fly; they glide. They have flat bodies and tails with a fold of skin (called a patagium) extending from front foot to hind foot on each side.

They travel by climbing high in a tree, then jumping off with all four legs, tail and patagium extended. This posture produces an airfoil that allows them to glide in a J-shaped arc for distances up to 150 feet. Usually a glide ends up at the base of another tree, followed by a climb to the top and another glide to a new tree. These glides can be quite spectacular.

Flying squirrels are generally friendly and easily tamed. They seldom bite if handled slowly and gently. A friend of mine once tamed a squirrel that went everywhere with him in his shirt pocket and seemed to enjoy the experience. Squirrels are gregarious and given to play with each other or by themselves.

Flying squirrels have been shown to have strong homing instincts. As an experiment some years ago, a squirrel live-trapped in the attic of a house in Nakoma was marked and taken to the Arboretum for release at a point one mile in a straight line from where it was caught. Six days later, the same marked squirrel was caught in the same attic.

Flying squirrels don't hibernate, although they are in-active in very cold weather. If there are flying squirrels in your neighborhood, they can be attracted to bird feeders or cobs of corn spiked to a tree trunk. Of course, the squirrels will only visit at night, so enough light to see them also should be provided.

I concur with mammalogist H.H.T. Jackson, who had this to say about the flying squirrel: "Its interesting and friendly habits and its beauty of form and action make it a desirable neighbor."

# THE GRAY GHOST OF LOST CITY

A woodcock brought me my best-ever look at a gray fox (*Urocyon cinereoargenteus*). Well, not literally, but if it hadn't been for the bird, I wouldn't have seen the fox.

One April evening in 1971, at the far east end of the Ar-boretum, I had set a mist net hoping to catch and band a male woodcock on his peenting (display) ground. As I watched the net from my seat under the sheltering branches of a nearby jack pine, I became aware of movement on the trail about 50 feet away. I realized that I was being watched by a gray fox. It stood on the trail at the edge of the Lost City woods, calmly staring at me. I had a wonderful close-up view of its pepper-and-salt coat tinged with buff, and its bushy, black-tipped tail.

Although red and gray foxes are about the same size, grays have shorter muzzles and longer legs than reds. The reds' coats are yellowish-red, not gray, and their tails are always tipped with white instead of black.

I guessed that the fox watching me was just starting out on its evening hunt. We both stayed perfectly still and appraised each other. Finally, several minutes later, the fox seemed to decide that I posed no threat and continued casually on its way down the trail. Grays are active mostly at night and are more secretive than their red cousins; hence they are less often seen by people.

Mammalogist W. H. Burt wrote that "the gray fox, although primarily a carnivore, is nearly as omnivorous as is man." Grays favor mice, rabbits and other small mammals as food, but also eat fleshy fruits, corn, insects and even a few birds. As a whole, however, their diet does not seem to seriously damage prey populations.

Gray foxes have been seen in nearly all Wisconsin counties, especially in the western driftless areas of the state. They are primarily found in woodlands where they keep dens under stumps, in hollow logs, under rock or wood piles, or in rocky crevices. The Arboretum woods offer good fox habitat and there probably is a gray or two still present, although seldom seen.

Grays have the unusual habit of regularly climbing trees to escape enemies or find food. They do this by jumping from limb to limb in trees with low-hung branches, or simply walking, cat-fashion, up the trunk of a leaning tree. Grays have been seen in trees up to 40 feet off the ground.

Yes, I did band the woodcock I was after, and I thought about the gray fox all the while I was doing it.

To top off the evening, just as I started driving the trail back to Arboretum headquarters, my headlights for an instant caught a gray fox walking toward the car, carrying what looked like a small rabbit. The fox immediately leaped into the bordering woods and disappeared. Was this the same gray I'd seen earlier? I don't know, but I would bet that somewhere in Lost City there was a litter of hungry gray fox pups.

## THE GARBAGE CAN THAT WALKS

The opossum (*Didelphis virginiana*) will never win a popularity contest. This grayish white mammal has prominent naked ears, a long, naked prehensile tail and is about the size of a large house cat. Its brain is small, its actions slow, and it gives an impression of being stupid.

Opossums are nocturnal, solitary wanderers who spend their daytimes sleeping in burrows, under brush piles, in hollow trees or in any other convenient hiding place. They do not hibernate in winter and often lose parts of their ears, tails or toes due to freezing. They're found statewide in Wisconsin, but primarily in the southern half of the state, including the Arboretum.

Opossums are true marsupials, the only one found north of Mexico in North America. Like kangaroos, females have an external pouch in which the young are carried from birth after a 13-day gestation period until weaned at about 80 days of age.

Perhaps opossums are best know for their habit of "playing possum," a phrase that to many of us means pretending to be ignorant or feigning death. Opossums do, in fact, often roll over and appear dead when under extreme stress, a behavior that is an involuntary but temporary nervous reaction to a threat the animal can't cope with.

Some years back, wildlife biologist George Knudsen studied the food habits of opossums in southern Wisconsin. He found that their diets included mammals, birds, invertebrates, reptiles, amphibians, fish, plants, garbage, and trash. The word "omnivorous" must have been invented to describe the opossum.

Mammalian foods included species from mice to cottontail rabbits to domestic swine. Domestic chicken was the most common of the bird remains in opossum stomachs.

The fact that many of these animals were too large, too fast or too strong for an opossum to catch and kill is evidence that opossums are primarily scavengers of dead animals. Confirmation of this was in the maggots and decayed condition of much flesh in opossum stomachs. It's hard to believe that an opossum can have more than a rudimentary sense of taste and smell.

Earthworms were especially important foods in the summer months. Some of the fish remains were obviously cleanings discarded by humans, and the remainder believed to be from dead fish found on land. The opossum is no fisherman in its own right. Fruits and vegetables, especially apples, were favored in season.

Human food waste such as cooked meat bones, potato peelings and cut carrot tops were often found in opossums stomachs. Even items such as leather, paper and twine occurred occasionally.

Despite the fact that this homely creature with its unattractive personality is almost literally a garbage can, its persistent ability to survive in a somewhat unfriendly environment must be admired. It may look and act stupid, but the opossum has succeeded where other life-forms have become extinct. It's not easy to argue against a winner.

## LOVE A BUG

It must be tough to be an insect. Hardly anyone likes them. They're food for all kinds of other animals, and even plants, such as pitcher plants. Most people equate "insect" with "pest," thinking first of mosquitoes, hornets, black flies, or other biters of humans and eaters of plants. Very few people have pet insects!

Even butterflies are only half-liked. The adults can be beautiful, but caterpillars on their way to being butterflies are detested when they munch on our growing garden vegetables.

Insects deserve a closer look. Worldwide, there are millions of species that have survived for millions of years. Many of our cherished wildflowers, such as May's trillium, puccoon, bellwort and lupine depend on a variety of insects for pollination.

Many insects have remarkable ways of life. Consider the familiar June bug, which could more accurately be called the May beetle. The adults usually emerge to feed and mate in May, when we hear them buzzing at screens, attracted to our lights at night. Their eggs are laid and hatch in soil covered with vegetation. The larvae spend three years underground, growing into the fat, white grubs we sometimes dig up in our gardens or find infesting our lawns. They feed on plant roots and decaying vegetation.

In winter they burrow deeper into the ground to stay below the frost line. In their third summer, they pupate underground. Adult beetles emerge the following spring to start their three-year life cycles all over again.

Maybe we need a Bug Appreciation Month to give these creatures their due respect.

# Up from the Mud — Abundant Amphibians

Tiger salamanders are not creatures that usually bring joy to the person who finds one. Homely, slow-moving, slimy-skinned adult salamanders give a first impression that they are lizards, but they're not. They are true amphibians adapted to live both in the water and on land, although their terrestrial habitats must be moist.

Wisconsin has eight species of salamanders. The tiger salamander (*Ambystoma tigrinum*) is one of our largest. It reaches about 13 inches in length, half of which is tail. It is found over most of the southern half of the state, except for the driftless area of the western counties. The species is widely distributed over the central United States.

Tigers can be recognized by their color pattern composed of many yellow blotches scattered over a dark brown or dark green body. These yellow spots vary widely in size and shape.

Adult tiger salamanders spend most of their lives underground. However, they appear on the surface, sometimes in great numbers, on warm rainy nights in early spring as they move toward their breeding ponds. They are often seen crawling across roads at this time. During their treks they occasionally manage to get into window wells, basements and ditches.

When my Madison home was new, it became a rite of spring for the kids next door to collect salamanders by the pail-full from the neighborhood window wells. Occasionally, I have seen salamanders at night crossing Arboretum Drive near the Teal Pond Creek, as well as at the Teal Pond itself.

Breeding areas can be woodland or prairie ponds, farm ponds, marshes and lakes. Courtship and egg-laying takes place under water. Eggs hatch in three to four weeks and young remain in the ponds until August, during which time they mature into their adult form, much as tadpoles transform into adult frogs. Another nocturnal movement takes place on warm, wet, late-summer nights as young of the year move toward a wintering area.

Tiger salamanders live in burrows of mammals, enlarged earthworm trails, and even in sewer and water-line tunnels. Proximity to people does not seem to be a hazard as long as a breeding pond is nearby. They feed on insects, earthworms, spiders and other invertebrates. While young are still in the aquatic larva stage, they eat primarily zooplankton. An unpleasant characteristic of tiger salamanders is that the slime on their bodies will irritate your eyes and sometimes your skin, too.

Zoologist R. C. Vogt wrote that even in suburban areas, "There may be hundreds of tiger salamanders under your feet, but you will never know it unless you see the fall or spring hordes or happen to excavate them."

# It's Not Easy Being Green

Among the unloved creatures of this world are frogs, and that's a shame. They deserve a better image for a variety of reasons. Frogs come in many colors and many sizes. Worldwide, there are hundreds of species. Even in Wisconsin, at least 13 species are recognized.

Frogs have interesting characteristics. They are great leapers, make surprising noises and can survive drastic seasonal changes in the weather. Some species are entirely aquatic, some live in grasslands, and some in forests. They eat tremendous numbers of insects and in turn are a food supply for many mammals, birds, fish and reptiles.

Given half a chance, their populations will prosper. On the other hand, a decline in their numbers usually is an early warning that some form of pollution is happening where they live. Frogs are quite sensitive to changes in their environments. A famous naturalist once said, "From the viewpoint of a frog, human beings serve no useful purpose."

Six frog species can be expected in the Arboretum — leopard frog, pickerel frog, spring peeper, chorus frog, gray tree frog and green frog.

May is a great month for listening to frog calls. At this time, the chorus frogs and spring peepers that tuned up in March and April are still calling and the late-spring species are just getting started.

Each species has a distinctive voice. At twilight, frogs begin to call intensely and will keep calling until the night gets too cold or morning light becomes too bright. A frog's call identifies its species just as a bird's song does. When calling, a frog doesn't have to be seen to be identified.

Only males call. Their function is to attract females for breeding, which takes place in or near water, even though some species spend the rest of the summer in forests or meadows.

You might enjoy making friends with frogs. As Pogo, the celebrated comic-strip philosopher, said, "Why turn a perfectly good frog into a prince?"

# THE BRIGHT SIDE OF BURNING

Wildfires started by natural causes such as lightning have occurred for centuries. As a result, many species of plants and animals have learned to use burned areas to their benefit.

This is one reason why controlled fires are regularly set by land managers to revitalize certain grasslands, forests, and wetlands.

Jack pine, one of Wisconsin's common conifers, is dependent on periodic fires to provide the high heat needed to open cones so seed may be released, to remove plant competition and to create a bed of ash suitable for seed germination.

The endangered Kirtland's warbler, a ground-nesting bird which presently nests only in scattered stands of six- to eight-foot high jack pines, is almost totally dependent on the pine stands regenerated by fire.

Anyone who has picked blueberries, blackberries or raspberries in central and northern Wisconsin may have discovered that recently burned forest edges provide the lushest growth and heaviest berry crops.

Burned-over aspen trees will sprout heavily from the roots, thus providing an abundant new food supply for deer, hares, and rabbits as well as good cover for ruffed grouse, songbirds, and small mammals.

Prairies owe their existence to periodic fires, as demonstrated each spring in the Arboretum. Prairie fires set by lightning or by Indians occurred long before European settlement of North America. The native prairie plants and animals have adapted to fire and require occasional burning if they are to prosper.

Even though a recently burned area looks desolate, in a surprisingly short time it will be hard to find much evidence of fire among the greenery.

## WHAT'S IN A NAME

Aldo Leopold wrote that "every profession keeps a small herd of epithets, and needs a pasture where they may run at large." Biologists are among the herders. One of their flock is a very interesting word — *commensalism*. My dictionary defines it as a "close association of two kinds of organisms in which one is benefited by the relationship and the other is neither benefited nor harmed."

One spring, an example occurred in the yard of a near-rural suburban home, where a mature white birch tree was attacked by a yellow-bellied sapsucker, a bird of the woodpecker family. Sapsuckers drill rows of small holes into the trunks of birches and other trees with sweet sap so they (the sapsuckers) may feed on the sap itself — and the insects that are attracted to it.

In this case, the sapsucker, while drilling holes and feeding, was joined by a ruby-throated hummingbird which also fed on the flowing juices and visiting insects. Later in the day, a red-eyed vireo feasted on the insects.

As evening came, nocturnal moths gathered at the still-flowing sap, and soon were preyed upon by several little brown bats. Later, a pair of flying squirrels visited the birch to share in its liquids and possibly its insects.

Thus there was multiple commensalism. A birch tree, attacked by one bird who was hungry but had no thought of others, ended up feeding three species of birds, two mammals and several kinds of insects, all in a period of about twelve hours. To the birds and mammals, the relationship was beneficial, but to the tree and the insect population, the episode had no apparent benefits or bad effects.

The message in all this is that possibilities for enjoying the out-of-doors are much greater than simply identifying and listing birds and flowers you see. The ways that animals and plants relate to each other are numerous, diverse, and not always easily apparent, but are identifiable if you'll take the time to carefully watch their behaviors. Such observations can be enjoyed at any season of the year.

SUMMER

# Phenology

June has arrived if the mosquitos are so bad you can't stay out in the backyard to watch the first fireflies of the season. Of course, there are lots of other natural events going on that mean June, too. The whole wild world is multiplying. It's a time of birdnestings, litter-rearings and wildflowerings. Animals reach peak numbers for the year. Abundant flowers precede the summer's seed crops.

Species native to south central Wisconsin include Canada mayflower and Solomon's-seal along woods edges, pucoon and wild indigo on the prairies, and spatterdock and blue flag in wetlands — to name a few.

But for a change of pace, take a closer look at some of the weeds we tend to dislike because of their aggressive habits. There is much color in the June blooms of butter-and-eggs, ox-eye daisy, heal-all (or self-heal), common St. Johnswort, wild parsnip and yarrow. The swatches of blue chicory and patches of orange day lilies along rural roadsides give an attractive aspect to what otherwise would be sterile miles of quackgrass.

All of these weeds are aliens brought to North America, primarily from Europe. Even though they may have flourished to the point of being pests, their flowers provide at least a small repayment for the trouble they may cause.

There is beauty to be found in the tiny blossoms of many small prairie plants such as green orchid, comandra, seneca snakeroot, yellow stargrass and northern bedstraw. Their flowers rival their larger relatives in everything but size, so use a hand lens to see them best.

Look for flowering shrubs in prairies and woods openings. New Jersey tea, blackberry, dogwood, wild rose, ninebark and bittersweet may be found. Even poison ivy has interesting flowers if you look closely, but don't touch them. There are some rather spectacular tree flowers, too. Keep an eye out for black and honey locusts, as well as catalpa trees. A catalpa covered with clusters of purple-dotted white flowers is a real eye-catcher.

June also offers the first wild fruits of the summer. Juneberry, wild strawberry, red-osier dogwood and Tartarian honeysuckle fruits are ripening and feeding wildlife. People, as well, will be feeding — on strawberries and juneberries.

The animal world is equally active. Listen for toads trilling near wet areas, sounding better than they look; interesting bird songs, such as red-eyed vireo and eastern pewee in the woods, or field sparrow and redwing on the prairies; the deep whir of wings at dusk as a male common nighthawk dives through the air in display flight.

Look for barn and tree swallows hawking insects over wetlands; white-tailed deer in their red summer coats, perhaps with a new fawn; black-spotted red milkweed beetles and big, black-banded, greenish-yellow caterpillars of monarch butterflies at home on common milkweed plants; half-grown young of gray squirrels, cottontail rabbits, chipmunks, opossums, ground squirrels and, with luck, red foxes.

While you're on a June ramble you may find your path occupied by a common snapping turtle, a creature to be watched, but not touched. They are pugnacious and have beaked jaws capable of severely injuring human flesh. Snappers are

Wisconsin's largest turtles and have toothed shells that grow to be about 16 inches long. They can be found in almost any aquatic site, but in June, females move to uplands where they dig cavities and lay eggs in the soft soil of road shoulders, sandy hills, dirt roads or riverbanks. The snapping turtle's name describes its temperament, so beware.

July finds the Arboretum prairies at their blooming best. Flowers abound. Larger species, such as prairie dock and purple coneflower are easy to see, but there are many equally spectacular small plants worth looking for: nodding onion — pink flower clusters droop from the top of a leafless stem; partridge pea — bright yellow flowers on plants with many very small leaflets; harebell — blue, bell-shaped flowers on thin, wiry stems with very narrow leaves; prairie loosestrife — yellow, five-petaled flowers and very narrow leaves; poppy mallow — deep red flowers on low plants that spread horizontally (they like dry prairies); side-oats grama — a dry-prairie grass, not a flower, but there's nothing else like it (the flowers and seeds grow only on one side of the stem).

Another mid-summer plant is marsh milkweed, a two-to-four-foot cousin of our common milkweed, that grows on wet ground. It has narrow leaves and flowers in deep pink clusters. Marsh milkweed is important to a bird, the willow flycatcher, which uses fibers stripped from the year-old stems as its main nesting material. This year's marsh milkweed stalks may well end up in a flycatcher nest next summer. These birds, once known as alder flycatchers, inhabit willow and elderberry thickets around the Arboretum's prairies and marshes. Their call, a sneezy "fitz-bew," is easy to recognize.

The Arboretum's Greene Prairie is usually home to an uncommon Wisconsin bird, the sedge wren. They're small birds, even for wrens, with stubby tails, streaked backs and crowns, and buffy underparts. They build domed nests of grass in the tops of prairie-grass clumps. Their distinctive dry, metallic song adds much to the prairie summer.

August is an in-between month. Plants and animals seem to be taking it easy between the "just over" stresses of their reproductive seasons and the "getting ready for" stresses of winter cold. August can be hot, dry, cool, humid, sometimes pleasant and often miserable — especially for hay fever sufferers. Even so, August has much to offer.

Many plants are still in flower. On woods' edges look for jewelweed (touch-me-not) with its exploding seed pods, brilliant red cardinal flower, and pink tick clover. On the Greene Prairie there are the tall flowers of the two Silphiums (compass plant and prairie dock), purple coneflower, blazing star, and gayfeather. Marsh flowers still evident include joe pye weed, boneset, turtlehead and ironweed.

August is also a fruiting season. Blackberries, wild cherries, and the big blue heads of common elderberry should be expected. Bur oak acorns will start to fall. They are the only acorns with caps that are gray and burry. Weeds are still in their prime, among them bull thistle, burdock, and giant ragweed.

Listen for the shrill buzzing of cicadas in the treetops. These noisy insects really epitomize the dog days of summer.

August even has some early migrant birds. Several sandpiper species, blue-winged teal, and American wigeon often can be found in small flocks late in the month in wet areas. Look for migrating common nighthawks from late afternoon to dark. Their white wing patches are easily seen as the widely scattered small flocks drift overhead.

# Plants, Animals
# & Other Things in Season

## Thoughts for a Summer Evening

A warm summer night is a great reminder of the abundant, diverse and complex life that surrounds us. The clicks and buzzes of hidden insects, the chirps of a restless cardinal, and the unidentified rustlings and scurryings in the flower garden all underscore how little we really know about the non-human world.

Even though we aren't sure if these sights and sounds are happening because of us or in spite of us, they provide reason to ponder what they are and how they came to be here.

The fireflies or "lightning bugs" flashing in the dark of suburban back yards are remarkable organisms. They're a kind of beetle. Both sexes can light up specialized organs in their abdomens, apparently as a means of attracting a mate. Even the larvae of fireflies are able to emit light, and are called "glow-worms."

What complex evolutionary trials and errors over how many millennia were needed to produce the fireflies' internal, light-producing chemical system? These built-in blinkers are fascinating to watch, but there must be a simpler way to attract the opposite sex.

The ringing cries and whirring wings of common nighthawks overhead in the June dusk raise other questions. The sounds mean that the birds quite likely are nesting on the flat graveled roof of a nearby building. Why is it that some birds quickly find ways to live with humans and some birds do not?

Nighthawks readily nest on roofs instead of the ground as they did in presettlement times. American robins and common grackles find our lawns and shrubbery much to their liking. Purple martins and house wrens quickly move into the man-made nest boxes we provide.

Why, though, do so many birds disappear when humans take over? Greater prairie chickens, bald eagles and upland sandpipers, for example, tolerate little disturbance from their human neighbors.

Recognizing wariness is one thing; knowing what causes it is quite another, and finding something we can do about it is always a challenge.

# AN INLAND SEA OF TALL GRASSES

Unlike their woodland counterparts, prairie wildflowers wait until mid-summer to put on their best show.

Think what it must have been like to see a Curtis Prairie that stretched for many miles in all directions with only an occasional small grove as the only trees in sight!

Early accounts by the first European explorers who broke out of the massive forests that lay between the Mississippi River and the Atlantic coast and gazed upon the unbroken vistas of the Midwest prairies are full of astonishment and wonder. These grasslands were new in their experience. The French explorers, among the first to reach the Mississippi Valley, had no term to describe what they saw, so they used their word "prairie," meaning meadow or grassland.

These newcomers were accustomed to small fenced crop fields, pastures and cultivated open parks. The vast American grasslands, which soon were called prairies universally, must have been an impressive new world for them to explore.

Botanists recognize three general types of prairies in Wisconsin, all of which are restricted to roughly the southern third of the state. Their classifications are based on soil type, soil moisture level and plant composition. Such distinctions are not sharp and intergrades between types are frequent, but typical examples are fairly easy to identify.

Many botanists or ecologists now add dry sand prairies as a separate type and this type is officially recognized by the DNR's Natural Areas section.

The driest prairies are called "xeric." Their plants are short and usually occupy very thin soils on steep limestone slopes, such as on the ends of the bluffs along the Mississippi River where they are sometimes nicknamed "goat prairies." Most prairie plants bloom after June 15, but the xeric prairies bloom earlier, with pasque flower, puccoons and birdfoot violet. Downy gentians are prominent in fall.

Mesic prairies, often called tall-grass prairies, have deep, moist soils and support vigorous, tall stands of grasses such as big bluestem (turkeyfoot) and Indian grass. Typical prairie wildflowers growing with the tall grasses include wild indigo, rattlesnake master and compass plant. Mesic prairies were the presettlement type throughout Illinois, Iowa and adjoining areas of their surrounding states.

Lowland prairies have wet, heavy soils and may be subject to seasonal flooding. Big bluestem is a major grass species in this prairie type, but other dominant grasses such as bluejoint and cordgrass are also found. Typical wildflowers of lowland prairies include bottle gentian, gayfeather, yellow stargrass and prairie dock. Because their wet soils do not warm up in early spring, few species bloom here before early June.

I find my joy in seeing a summer prairie in full bloom, tempered by the nearly total destruction of the native midwest prairies following settlement. The millions of original prairie acres have been reduced to pitifully small remnants along railroad rights-of-way and in odd field corners.

Fortunately, many of these tiny patches are being preserved and restored, but the great glories of the Midwest "sea of grass" never will be seen again.

## BEWARE THE WILD PARSNIP

Have you ever suffered the medical mouthful called phytophotodermatitis? It's that itching, blistered skin and persistent rash you can get from contact with certain unfriendly plants. Severe cases may require hospitalization and leave permanent scars.

On the other hand, some people seem to have a natural immunity to such afflictions. Individual tolerances vary widely. While one person bears scars from a past encounter with a plant, another reports pulling it up with her bare hands without consequences. It's prudent to avoid all plants known to cause such reactions, regardless of what you think about your own immunities.

Contact dermatitis is a well-known problem with a long list of culprits. They range from poison ivy (Rhus radicans), its cousin poison sumac (Rhus vernix), stinging marsh nettles (Laportea canadensis) and wood nettles (Urtica dioica) and to many that are less well known, including eight species of spurge (Euphorbia).

Certain plants, including wild parsnip (Pastinaca sativa), cause trouble due to their unique phytophototoxic characteristics. It is the juice from the bruised leaves, flowers or broken stems of this plant that does the damage, photosensitizing the skin so that exposure to sunlight produces rash and water blisters like those of a severe burn, ultimately leaving brown scars that can last for years — or permanently. The symptoms will not appear until the contacted skin gets into sunlight — sometimes days after the encounter. Sometimes trouble may be averted by keeping parsnip-touched skin out of the sun until you have washed well with soap and water.

Wild parsnip's hazards do not seem to be widely known. Dane County naturalist Wayne Pauly found it thriving in schoolyards where he had gone to talk on poisonous plants. Mowed along with the grass, it then causes the symptoms that mystify parents, teachers and even doctors.

Wild parsnip has become well established on heavier soils in most of Wisconsin. It flourishes on disturbed ground, in old fields, unused garden patches and roadsides. It grows to a height of two to five feet and has a coarse, hollow, fluted stalk with small yellow flowers appearing in late spring in a flat-headed umbel. The flowers produce large, flattened oval seeds. The leaves are compound and toothed.

In origin, it is the plain old garden parsnip brought over from Europe and now escaped from cultivation. Its fleshy first-year root is said to be edible if dug from fall to early spring, but by the time it flowers, the entire plant becomes poisonous, both when eaten and touched.

The best way to get rid of this big, bad weed is to cut it down in its full bloom, before it sets seeds. Timing is all-important. If cut too early, the plant may resprout, although it does not regrow from the root as does, for instance, dandelion. A freshly disturbed site formerly without parsnip can be controlled by persistent cutting for about four years, Wayne says, but a site occupied for years by this weed may take decades of control efforts.

Wayne points out that plant cycles often go their mysterious ways despite human intervention, and it can be difficult to assess whether it is the planned measures that discourage a weed or a natural event.

Arboretum ecologist Virginia Kline had evidence of this; she reported success eliminating the parsnip from a small area in Curtis Prairie, but knows another part of the prairie where it seemed to disappear spontaneously.

No plant is all bad; the wild parsnip earns its place in the scheme of nature as a primary host plant for the black swallowtail butterfly caterpillar. You can identify the caterpillar by touching its tail; it will rear up, project its horns, and emit a distinctive odor. But don't touch its host, the troublesome wild parsnip.

## ORCHIDS IN THE ARBORETUM

What image comes to mind when someone mentions orchids? Most of us see showy, colorful flowers festooning a tropical forest, or perhaps a corsage for Mothers' Day or the senior prom. However, such blossoms are only a small part of the orchid family, which is large and cosmopolitan with about 7,000 species.

Several dozen species are native to Wisconsin, and at least seven can be found in the Arboretum. Some are small and inconspicuous, while two of my favorites, the white and small yellow lady's-slippers, are easily visible when blooming on Greene Prairie in early June. Both species grow to approximately one foot tall.

Lady's-slippers are in the genus Cypripedium, a name that is a Latinized form of Greek words meaning "shoe of Venus." This name is descriptive of the inflated sac-like or slipper-shaped petal called the lip. Three other lady's-slippers (pink, showy, and ram's-head) are native to Wisconsin but are not found in the Arboretum.

White lady's-slippers are officially a threatened species in our state. They once grew by the thousands in low prairies and open meadows, but agriculture, wetland drainage and urban development have eliminated all but about a dozen scattered small populations in southern Wisconsin. Large yellow lady's-slippers are somewhat more common in bogs and moist woods throughout the state and may reach two feet in height.

Yellows are numerous enough in Door County to have been named the official county wildflower by the Door County Board.

Lady's-slippers have unusual pollination mechanisms. Insects, usually wild bees, attracted to the flowers crawl into the inflated lip in search of nectar. Finding none, they have difficulty crawling back out because of an arrangement of stiff hairs on the inside of the lip. The only route out of the flower forces the insect to rub against the sticky pollen structures, thus loading it up for its visit to another lady's-slipper.

Lady's-slipper seeds are very tiny, almost like dust, and very abundant. They may lie in the soil for several years before germinating. Once a white or yellow lady's-slipper seed sprouts, plants slowly increase in size each year, but do not flower until they are at least eight years old, and sometimes not until their sixteenth year. Individual plants may live 20 years or more.

Yellow and white lady's-slippers seldom if ever grow well under cultivation because of their specialized soil requirements. To prosper, their roots must be in contact with specific hair-like soil fungi. The fungi convert carbohydrates and proteins in the soil into a liquid form which is then taken in by the lady's-slipper seedlings, which have no stored food of their own.

Transplanting lady's-slippers into a home garden is a waste of superb native wildflowers and the gardener's time because the critical soil components the plants require are seldom present. Lady's-slippers should be enjoyed where they belong — in the wild.

# PARSLEY GOES SOUTHWESTERN

Sometimes I don't understand wildflowers. Why are midwestern prairies home to a plant that looks like an escapee from an Arizona desert? It has leaves like a yucca, pale green foliage and many spines. Altogether, it seems out of place in a prairie setting, even though it is a Wisconsin native and is common in the Arboretum prairies.

This plant is rattlesnake master (Eryngium yuccifolium), a member of the parsley family, which makes it a cousin of better-known species such as sweet Cicely, Queen Anne's lace and the carrots in your vegetable garden.

Another name for it is button snake-root. It grows three to four feet tall from a basal rosette of long (up to three feet), sword-shaped leaves which are edged with sharp spines. If you must handle it, do so with care.

Its tall, stiff stem is topped by several round flower heads. Each head is composed of many closely massed tiny white flowers which are viewed best with a hand lens. At full bloom in mid-summer, the flower clusters look like fuzzy white balls, and have a nice fragrance. After flowering, heads become hard and prickly to the touch.

The leaves of rattlesnake master, in addition to being spiny, have rows of hardened cells on their edges and along their midribs. These seem to prevent attacks by leaf-eating insects which find the hardened leaf-edges where they begin feeding to be inedible. Another leaf characteristic is the presence of sunken pores which help to reduce water loss during droughts.

Rattlesnake master has a place in herbal medicine. This plant and others in its genus were widely used by Native Americans as a cure for poisonous snake bites. To that end, a concoction of leaves and stems was brewed and taken internally. Prairie pioneers learned of it and it became a widely accepted remedy.

Obviously, the name rattlesnake master is related to its perceived effect on snakes. Folklore says that all snakes avoid it, but there seems to be a difference of opinion about this. Author John Madson recounted a story told to him by an elderly prairie farmer that "rattlesnake master in a 'wild hay' field was a sure sign that massasauga rattlers were present. His grand-dad had told him that, so it had to be true."

If you have a prairie garden, rattlesnake master is a perennial that will grow nicely on loamy soils in full sun. It is available as seeds or plants through several prairie nursery catalogs.

# Mid-Summer Milkweeds

The mid-summer flower show in and near the Arboretum prairies includes five species of milkweeds. All are native plants in the genus Asclepias (named for an ancient Greek physician) characterized by fluffy, winged seeds borne in pods. With one exception, all have sticky white juices in their stems — hence their common name.

The species most often seen is common milkweed (A.syriaca). It is a stout plant with broad leaves and stems up to five feet tall topped with one or more rounded, tennis-ball-sized cluster of pale pink flowers. If you've never smelled one, you will be surprised by their pleasant fragrance. Both the young leaves and flower clusters are edible when properly cooked.

Two insects likely to be found on milkweed are the bright red milkweed beetle, which has four black spots on each wing and long antennae, and the caterpillar stage of the monarch butterfly. This large, greenish-yellow caterpillar has prominent black bands and two horns at each end. In fact, the monarch is sometimes called the milkweed butterfly.

Marsh or swamp milkweed (A.incarnata) grows in wetland sites. Its leaves are narrower and its flower clusters are more red and less round than those of its common cousin. The silky outer covering that can be stripped from the last year's flower stalks is a favorite nest material of willow flycatchers and goldfinches.

Dry prairies are the home of butterfly weed (A.tuberosa), a short, shrubby-looking milkweed topped by brilliant orange flower clusters. This plant is attractive to several species of butterflies as well as people, and does not have milky juices. Butterfly weed was once know as pleurisy root because of its reputed medicinal value.

Look for bluntleaf milkweed (A.amplexicaulis) along the prairie-woods edge. It resembles common milkweed, but its leaves are wavy rather than flat and clasp the stem. Its flowers are pinkish yellow in a sparser cluster than that of common milkweed.

Whorled or white milkweed (A.verticillata) is another short species (one or two feet) with white flowers and whorled, grasslike leaves. The flower clusters are quite small and you'll need a close look to see the typical milkweed flower structure. The seed pods are not large, but once their seeds have flown they make good additions to winter bouquets.

## PRAIRIE PURPLE

The mid-summer splashes of color on the Arboretum prairies are highlighted by the three-foot-tall brightness of purple coneflowers. Their large, dark-purple centers are surrounded by lighter pink or purple ray flowers in a drooping, daisy-like bloom.

The Arboretum prairies have two look-alike species. The most common type is not even a native of Wisconsin. Its Latin name is Echinacea purpurea. Echinacea is from a Greek word meaning "hedge hog," which was given in reference to the spiny-looking center of the flower. Purpurea refers to the color purple.

The natural range of E. purpurea is just south of Wisconsin, but it was transplanted to the Arboretum in the early years of development and has been very successful, even to the point of repressing the growth of other prairie species around it. Because it grows so easily, several horticultural varieties are available for home gardens.

The second purple coneflower is named E. pallida, a name that refers to the paler ray flowers when compared to E. purpurea. It's ray flowers always droop, in contrast to E. purpurea which often has horizontal ray flowers.

It is a rare Wisconsin native and is on the Wisconsin threatened species list. Its leaves are narrow—about an inch wide, while E. purpurea has broader leaves.

E. pallida is found in both moist and dry prairies. It was first discovered in Wisconsin near Madison in 1855, but hasn't been seen there since 1935, except for the Arboretum transplants. However, there are recent records from remnant rail-road prairies in Rock, Green and Grant counties. It has none of the weedy characteristics of E. purpurea.


# THE MAGNIFICENT SIX

Cup plant, rosinweed, ox-eye, Jerusalem artichoke, beggar-ticks and prairie coneflower are six summer flowers that grow in the Arboretum.

Do you know how they are related to each other? While their common names don't show it, they're all members of the Sunflower tribe in the Daisy or Aster family (in Latin, the Asteraceae, formerly the Compositae).

There are other members of the tribe you can look for in the Arboretum. In the prairies, woodland edges or wetlands you might find black-eyed Susan, Coreopsis, branched cone-flower, purple coneflower, naked-stem sunflower and woodland sunflower.

Their tribe is a large one. It includes such weeds as cocklebur and ragweed, and such cultivated species as zinnias and the domestic sunflowers that produce the seed for your bird feeders.

The flowers of all the species in the group are similar in structure, but the blossoms come in different sizes. What looks like a single flower is really many small flowers grouped tightly together. In the center is a rounded cluster of tiny tubular disk flowers, which are surrounded by a ring of strap-like ray flowers that look like single petals. A hand lens will give you a good look at all this. Most sunflowers are yellow, although purple coneflower is an obvious exception. As a group, sunflowers are tall and robust.

Two prominent prairie species in the Silphium genus of the sunflower tribe are compass plant and prairie dock. Both may grow to more than eight feet tall. Both have leaves that usually are oriented so that only the edge faces the hot noonday sun. The leaves of prairie dock are broad, heart-shaped and about two feet long, and clustered at the base of the plant. The basal leaves of the compass plant are similar in size but are deeply cleft. There are a few smaller leaves on the flowering stalk.

Aldo Leopold wrote, "Silphium first became a personality when I tried to dig one up to move to my farm … After half an hour of hot grimy labor the root was still enlarging, like a great vertical sweet potato. As far as I know, that Silphium root went clear through to bedrock."

Another interesting sunflower is Jerusalem artichoke, a resident of moist soils on low ground. It's a large plant, growing from four to 10 feet tall with many short branches. It has large edible tubers that are sweet, nutritious and starchy. Author Euell Gibbons says tubers should be dug after frost but before the ground freezes. They can be cooked as you would potatoes, or eaten raw as a salad vegetable.

Jerusalem artichoke is native to the upper Mississippi River valley, but Indians had these plants under cultivation on the east coast when European colonists first arrived. When colonists sent them back home, they called it "sunflower artichoke." This was corrupted somehow into Spanish for sunflower — girasole — and through twisted English translation became "Jerusalem," even though the species originated in the middle of North America.

# A NOISY NEIGHBOR

The hot afternoons of mid-summer can be noisy. On some days the shrill, rasping cries of insects hidden in the tree tops are the loudest and most persistent sounds to be heard out of doors. The producer of this racket is the cicada, a two-inch-long, heavy bodied, clear-winged, black and green member of the insect order Homoptera.

There are several species of cicadas, all similar in form and habits. Other members of their order include aphids, leaf hoppers and spittle insects. Cicadas are sometimes called dog-day harvest flies, or locusts, although they are not related to the true locusts, which are in the same order as grasshoppers and crickets.

Adult cicadas lay eggs in slits they cut in twigs of the trees they inhabit. The eggs hatch in several weeks and shortly there-after the nymphs drop to the ground and burrow into the soil where they may remain as nymphs for up to 17 years, depend-ing on the species.

While underground, the larvae or grubs live on juices they get from the roots of plants. When they finally come above ground, they cling to the bark of trees or to other objects until their pupal shell splits and the adult form emerges. Adult cica-das also feed on plant juices, but are not considered harmful to their host trees.

The cicada's loud, grating calls are produced by a compli-cated set of internal membranes and small cavities which, by muscular contractions, are made to resonate against specialized parts of the body wall. This intricate system makes a cicada one of the world's noisiest insects. Some entomologists believe cicadas are deaf, because they continue to sing even in the presence of a variety of sharp noises, including gunshots.

## NOT ALL MOSQUITOES BITE

No matter what the spring weather has been, sooner or later the mosquitoes will catch up with us. And there are a lot of them to do the chasing, since mosquitoes are found world-wide, with about 150 species in eleven genera in North America.

It could be worse; not all mosquitoes bite. Some species feed on nectar and other plant juices, while even among the biting kinds it is only the females that require a meal of blood from a vertebrate animal in order to produce eggs. Males will not bite you. Think what it would be like if all mosquitoes needed to probe your bloodstream.

Mosquitoes as a group are part of the order of insects called Diptera, and as such are relatives of house flies, midges, and crane flies, among others.

Mosquitoes have been intensively studied for many years, mostly because of their pest status and disease-carrying propensities. Malaria, yellow fever and encephalitis are among the better-known afflictions mosquitoes transmit in some areas.

Mosquitoes have widely varying habits, although all of them lay their eggs in or at the edge of water. The eggs hatch and stay in water through all the larval stages, becoming airborne only at maturity.

Some species seldom get more than a few feet from where they originate. Others are believed to fly up to 50 miles in search of a meal of blood. Some species are partial to puddles in tree holes or on the forest floor, or even in the tubular leaves of pitcher plants.

Mosquito larvae are the "wrigglers" often seen in standing water. In fact, the eggs of some species have better hatching rates in temporary run-off puddles than they do in more permanent waters.

The larvae feed on organic debris and bacteria both at the surface of the water and on the bottom. They have breathing tubes at the rear of their bodies which enable them to take in oxygen at the surface.

The greatest enemy of mosquitoes is hot, dry weather that eliminates their breeding pools before larvae can mature. However the eggs of many species can stay dormant two or three years, until the next flood comes along and the eggs have adequate water in which to hatch and grow. Some species live only for a week as adults, while others can survive all summer.

Entomologist Dennis Lemkuhl wrote that "mosquitoes are one of the unfortunate productions of nature which make life miserable." That just about says it all.

# A PREHISTORIC PREDATOR

More than 300 million years ago, even before the first dinosaur, a major predator appeared on this earth. It has prospered until this day. Multiplying its kind, it has gained worldwide distribution, and at present Wisconsin has at least 108 of the 580 species known to inhabit the United States and Canada.

This creature will attack anything it thinks it can eat with its strong serrated jaws. Its four wings and extra-large eyes with nearly 360-degree vision enable it to catch and eat its prey on the fly.

In case you haven't guessed, these master killers are dragonflies, the big game of the insect world. Some people call them "darning needles" or "mosquito hawks."

It is said that if they can get close enough, they will sew your lips and eyelids together. This bit of folklore is untrue, however. Dragonflies do not attack people; insects are their main food. Investigators have claimed that dragonflies will do a better job of controlling mosquitos than purple martins or little brown bats. Another bit of native wisdom shared by many fishermen is that if a dragonfly alights on your fishing rod it will bring you a good catch.

One of the dragonflys' fascinating characteristics is their flying ability. They can stop, start, and change direction instantaneously. Dragonflies are so good at this that the U.S. Air Force is trying to figure out how they can fly in a style that conventional wisdom says should be impossible.

Dragonflies are found near lakes, streams, ponds and marshes, or wherever there is permanent, clean water. Pollution threatens their survival, and their numbers decrease as water quality deteriorates.

They spend 90 percent or more of their lives under water as aquatic nymphs which eat anything that moves, including tadpoles and small fish.

Eventually, nymphs crawl out of the water and, on a rock or plant stem, shed their exoskeletons ("skins"). The change to adult form is soon completed when the body and wings expand and dry out. Adults, in turn, mate and lay eggs in the water; their life cycle then repeats itself.

Wisconsin and Illinois are home to one of the rarest of North American dragonflies, the Hines emerald. In Wisconsin it is found only in Door County, and it is being considered for listing as the first dragonfly to be protected by the U.S. Endangered Species Act.


# LOUD, BUT LUCKY

Summer nights can be noisy. Insects, a few birds, thunder, the neighbor's yowling cats, all contribute to a decibel level that might disturb your sleep. One of the most common, persistent and loudest of the noisemakers is an insect, the cricket.

Hundreds of species of crickets have been described in North America. However, there seems to be disagreement among entomologists about just how many species deserve recognition. At any rate, the most abundant one in our area is the black field cricket. These insects are about an inch long, with strong back legs and long antennae. They are widely distributed in the United States. Although they have wings, they rarely fly, but are good jumpers.

They are found in crop fields, pastures, lawns, roadsides, woods and houses, although crickets inside buildings are most apt to be another similar and common species, the European house cricket.

A cricket's life begins as one of up to 300 eggs laid by a female in soil during late summer and fall. Eggs winter underground and hatch in spring. Adult crickets hibernate in late fall, but seldom survive the winter. A year-old cricket is a rarity.

Crickets feed on lots of things — plant tissues, dead insects, seeds, leather, paper, and old cloth, especially if the cloth is stained by food or perspiration. They are capable of doing considerable damage in storage places.

Adult crickets spend their days in a shallow burrow beneath a stone, clod of dirt or a tuft of plants. They are most active after dark, and that is when males begin their nightly serenading of potential mates. Their familiar chirps also can be heard occasionally in the daytime. Females don't sing.

A male cricket has a heavy vein with a rough surface at the front of each wing. The upper side of a wing is used as a scraper and produces sound when it is rubbed across the rough vein of the other wing, as a bow is drawn across a violin. This performance occurs with both wings elevated so that wing membranes can act as sounding boards. The pitch of their chirps is slightly higher than the highest octave on a piano. Air temperature influences chirping rates; the warmer the night, the faster they chirp.

Folklore has it that a pet cricket will ward off evil spirits or bring good luck or both. For those who wish to test this possibility, crickets are easy to keep in captivity. Put a layer of sand in a fruit jar, add a small bottle cap for water, a cricket, and cover the jar opening with mosquito netting. Feed bits of lettuce, dry oatmeal, melon or chicken bone and your cricket should be happy. Perhaps you will be, too.

# BENEFICIAL BATS

Whenever I see a bat flitting around my backyard at dusk, I wonder why so many people are afraid of these flying furry creatures. Bats are too often said to attack humans, to make nests in your hair, to drink blood from babies' necks, to always carry rabies, and to be blind (as in "blind as a bat"). Bats are accused of being evil companions of witches, devils and imps; just look at how often bats are part of Halloween decorations.

Of course, none of this litany of fear is true. Wisconsin's bats do not bite people unless they are captured and need to defend themselves. Even then, their bites are not serious. There are three blood-sucking species (vampires) in Latin America, but they feed on livestock, not people. Rabies is now believed to occur in less than half of one percent of bats, which is not a public health problem.

Bats are not hated worldwide. Chinese artists portray bats as symbols of good luck, happiness and long life. Legends from some of the Pacific Islands describe bats as heroes.

Bats are the only mammals capable of true flight. (Flying squirrels glide, but can't sustain flight.) Bat bodies bear fine fur, but their ears and wing membranes are hairless. Their wings are modified front legs on which bones of the forepaws have become much elongated into flexible supports for the wing membranes. In effect, bats fly by waving their equivalent of other mammals' front legs.

About one thousand species of bats are found around the world. In Wisconsin, eight kinds are known and five of these have been found in the Arboretum. The little brown bat (Myotis lucifugus), big brown bat (Eptesicus fuscus) and red bat (Lasiurus borealis) are the species most often seen here. Others are the long-eared bat (Myotis keenii) and hoary bat (Lasiurus cinereus). These five range in body length from three to five inches, with wing spans of nine to 15 inches.

Because they fly mostly at night, there are more bats around than you might think. Little brown, big brown and long-eared bats spend the daytime hanging by their feet in caves, deep clefts in rock faces, hollow trees, and in the nooks and crannies around buildings. Red and hoary bats roost in trees. The little brown is the most numerous bat in our area.

Bats produce high-frequency sounds that enable them to navigate and communicate in the air. They are not blind and can see everything but color. Their echo-location systems are so sensitive that in complete darkness they can detect a human hair in their flight path. In this respect, they are many times more efficient than similar systems built by humans.

Wisconsin bats eat only insects. They do a much better job of mosquito control than purple martins or those electronic bug-zappers. Research has shown that little brown bats may eat

600 mosquitos an hour. Thus a colony of several hundred bats is capable of consuming more than a million mosquitos a night.

Bats in general feed on all kinds of agricultural pests, such as grain and cutworm moths, potato beetles, corn borers and grasshoppers, as well as other flying insects. Red bats are partial to moths and are often seen around street lights. Big brown bats seem to prefer beetles.

Bat expert Merlin Tuttle has written, "Bats are important indicators of a healthy environment, and they should be a welcome part of our neighborhoods. Like canaries in a mine, they serve as early warning systems for dangerously high pesticide and pollution levels. The occasional nuisance situation can be remedied, often easily, without having to fear or declare war on bats. Their presence is clearly beneficial — they will leave you alone, but mosquitos won't!"

## Name That Song

Part of the fun of bird watching is bird listening — knowing how a bird sounds as well as how it looks. Listening skill isn't especially hard to acquire; mainly it takes practice to learn birds by sound. Many of our summer-resident birds are still singing in the early mornings of the first half of July, so in mid-summer there is still time to do some learning by ear.

One helpful tool is translating a bird's call or song into spoken words. People who write field guides must think this is fun (and so should we), as their books are full of such phrases.

Most everyone knows that Canada geese honk, American crows caw and mallards quack. There are birds whose names mimic their sounds. Common bobwhites whistle "Bob White, poor Bob White." Phoebes sing "fee-bee." Whip-poor-wills sing just that. Black-capped chickadees call "chick-a-dee-dee-dee." Black-billed cuckoos sing "coocoocoo-coocoocoo-coocoocoo." Veerys sing a downward-slurring "veer, veer, veer, veer."

It helps to learn that an American robin sings "cheerily, cheer up," because a field guide might tell you that a rose-breasted grosbeak sounds "like a robin that has taken voice lessons," or that a scarlet tanager sings "like a robin with a sore throat."

Many other species sing phrases that are easy to remember. For example: Rufous-sided towhee — "drink your tea"; white-throated sparrow — "old Sam Peabody, Peabody"; ovenbird — "teacher, teacher, teach"; northern cardinal — "what cheer, cheer, cheer"; black throated green warbler — "Lucy, see, see, Suzy"; or chestnut-sided warbler — "see, see, see, see Miss Beecher."

Of course, some bird songs are so complicated they become untranslatable and thus are a challenge to their hearers. House wrens have been described as having "a gurgling song in a musical burst;" song sparrows as singing "variable notes, some musical, some buzzy;" purple finches as giving "a fast, lively warble;" and yellow-headed blackbirds as sounding "like the rusty hinges on a gate."

# BEAUTY AND THE BIRD

If there ever was a contest to pick Wisconsin's most beautiful bird, I'd vote for the cedar waxwing. Its sleek plumage is a delicate composition of shaded browns and grays with pale yellow under-tail coverts and a black mask through the eyes. These basic colors are set off by three attractive features — a conspicuous swept-back crest, a yellow band at the end of its tail, and waxy red tips on its secondary wing feathers. Altogether, waxwings are very stylish birds.

The wing tips that give the bird its name resemble red sealing wax, and are extensions of feather shafts that seem to reduce wear on individual feathers. The number of red tips varies from bird to bird. They may appear on all nine secondaries or only on one or two.

Cedar waxwings in Wisconsin are common migrants and summer residents. A few spend the winter with us. They nest later than most birds. Active nests have been recorded from late June to early September. Thick shrubs and small trees, especially white cedars, are favored nest sites. Waxwings are sometimes called "cedarbirds" because of their fondness for cedar trees.

Waxwings dote on fruit. Mountain ash, highbush cranberry, apple, juneberry, and both wild and cultivated cherries are examples. While about 80 percent of their diet is vegetable, they often hawk insects from a high perch like flycatchers.

These gentle birds have two unusual behaviors. One is their sociability and the other is the irregularity of their whereabouts in fall and winter. Except when nesting, you seldom see one waxwing at a time. They love to travel about in restless flocks, sometimes just a few birds, but sometimes numbering in the hundreds.

Where birds will be between breeding seasons is unpredictable. Ornithologist Sam Robbins has pointed out four winter patterns that may appear in Wisconsin: virtually absent from the state, scattered flocks statewide, present only in southern and central counties, and present only in the eastern half of the state. Waxwings just don't travel like other migratory birds.

Occasionally, a Canadian cousin of our cedar waxwing, the Bohemian waxwing, may show up in a winter flock of cedarbirds. Bohemians are slightly larger and grayer, with no yellow undersides, but with rusty under-tail coverts and white wing bars. Their winter visits to Wisconsin are just as mysterious as their cousins'. Some years they may be extremely scarce, while in other years flocks of a hundred or more may appear.

Ornithologist A.C. Bent described a waxwing as "an elegant bird, a well-dressed gentleman in feathers, a Beau Brummel among birds ... Softly blended shades of modest grays and browns form a most pleasing combination of colors. He is a gentleman in appearance ..." And I might add that female waxwings should share this praise; they cannot be told apart from males by their appearance.

# Who's "hoo" Among Wisconsin Owls

A great memory of my childhood is lying in bed and heading for sleep while listening to the gentle whinnying call of the screech owls nesting in the big maple tree in our side yard.

Once heard, this song will stick with you. Each summer, when our pair had their five or six young off the nest, for several evenings just at dusk the whole owl brood would perch along the peak of our neighbor's roof and wait to be fed sparrows or large earthworms or insects, or whatever else their parents would bring them.

Screech owls are one of 12 species of owls found in Wisconsin, and one of three species known to have nested in the Arboretum. The others are great horned and barred owls. Long-eared and northern saw-whet owls are occasional winter visitors to the Arboretum and may have nested here in earlier years.

The snowy, great gray, northern hawk and boreal owls are irregular winter visitors to Wisconsin, although in recent years a few nests of great grays have been discovered in our northwestern counties.

Short-eared owls are open-country birds that hang around grasslands in central and northern Wisconsin. They are more active in the daytime than any other of our owls.

Barn owls are pale-plumaged owls with a white, heart-shaped face and dark eyes. They are an endangered species in Wisconsin. They favor old buildings, barns, silos and church steeples as nesting sites.

The burrowing owl is the least common of Wisconsin's owls. This is a western prairie species that nests underground and seldom reaches east of Iowa and Minnesota. It is classed as a casual migrant in our state.

All 12 owls are predators, living almost entirely on other animals. Mice, rabbits, songbirds, large insects and other invertebrates are popular prey. Their predatory habits are enhanced by large and strong feet with sharp talons, hooked bills, and wings with feathering that makes their flight almost soundless.

The great horned owl is the champion killer of them all. It will attack anything that moves which it thinks will make a meal. Cottontail rabbits, squirrels, duck, muskrats, even domestic chickens, cats, and small dogs are in their diet. "Tiger of the woods" is a well-earned nickname for this species.

Barred owls and great horned owls are somewhat similar in appearance, but they have two characteristics to look for. The great horned has two long feathers on each side of its head (hence "horned"), while the barred does not. Also, the barred and barn owls have dark eyes, while all the other species, including the great horned, have yellow eyes.

An owl's ability to see and hunt in the dark is assisted by its flattened face on which feathers form a reflecting facial disk, and forward-looking eyes which provide binocular vision.

Owls in general, and great horned owls in particular, have been persecuted in past years because of their reputations as killers of game and poultry, but they are still with us. They are to be admired as survivors of the human race. I hope the song of the screech owl will always be heard.


## AN AMPHIBIAN PRINCE

When I went out to our vegetable patch to see how the tomato plants were faring, I discovered that the weeds were winning. In disgust, I kicked at a clod of dirt, but didn't follow through because the clod suddenly hopped about six inches to one side. My scorn turned to a smile when I realized that the jumper was an American toad (*Bufo americanus*).

Every garden deserves a toad. Yes, they're not charismatic, sort of ugly, and most people find them unpleasant. Such feelings are a bad rap. Toads are really beneficial critters. Their diet is mainly invertebrate animals, including such garden pests as beetles, caterpillars, snails and slugs.

Toads spend their days huddled under plants that keep them out of the sunlight. Most of their foraging is done at night. You might find one attracted to the insects around your yard light.

Toads are members of the same order as frogs and are found statewide in Wisconsin. They're about three inches long with a chunky build. Their skin is warty and brownish in color. Their legs are short and they often walk as well as hop.

Toads use any kind of still water for breeding, from rainwater puddles to ponds and lakes. Their spring mating call is a loud, 30-second trill all on one pitch. It's very easy to recognize.

Eggs are laid underwater and hatch out as black tadpoles with fat bodies and narrow tails. Tadpoles often form large schools in shallow water, a habit not found among frogs. When tadpoles reach their adult form, they leave the water and disperse through neighboring uplands for the summer.

Handling toads will not give you warts, as folk lore would have you believe. Nor do toads sit on mushrooms as the name "toadstool" implies. However, they're not friendly to handle. Toads have two glands just behind their heads which secrete a liquid that can irritate mucous membranes and cause rashes or a burning sensation when it touches your skin.

Few animals eat adult toads because of their toxic skins and apparent bad taste. One exception is the hognose snake, which seems to be immune to toad toxicity.

I don't care how homely a toad may be as long as it will decimate the bugs in my garden


## SNAKES AND STEREOTYPES

Few people are fond of snakes. Too many of us think the only good snake is a dead snake. Whether you love 'em or not, summers always bring us snakes.

I have seen at least four species in the Arboretum: Brown (sometimes called DeKay's) snake, red-bellied snake, milk snake and, by far the most common both here and throughout Wisconsin, the eastern garter snake. There may be other resident species that are less abundant. In any event, none of them are poisonous.

Let's look at the garter snake as an example to see why snakes seldom deserve their bad reputation. Garter snakes (and all other species) do not swallow their young, or charm their prey before eating it, or use their tongue for a stinger, or milk cows, or seek vengeance if their mate is killed, or roll down hills with their tails in their mouths, or do other weird things folklore accuses them of. In fact, for all practical purposes, garter snakes are harmless and useful.

Garter snakes are slender, and adults grow to two feet in length. They have three yellowish lengthwise stripes on a dark background. They live everywhere — lowland forests, marshes, meadows, river banks and prairies, as well as parks and vacant lots in urban areas. They come out of hibernation in early spring to breed. Young are born alive in late summer, as many as 70 at one time. One author estimated that a female will bear about 450 young in her lifetime.

When handled, garter snakes give off a nasty-smelling musk that can stay with you for a long time. They will sometimes bite, but more a nip than a serious chomp.

Garter snakes are good swimmers and hunt for food both day and night. They feed on other animals (frogs, toads, salamanders, earthworms, fish, young birds, mice, insects) and in turn are preyed upon by raccoons, skunks, hawks and other birds, and even snakes of larger species.

Being a garter snake seems like a hard life.

FALL

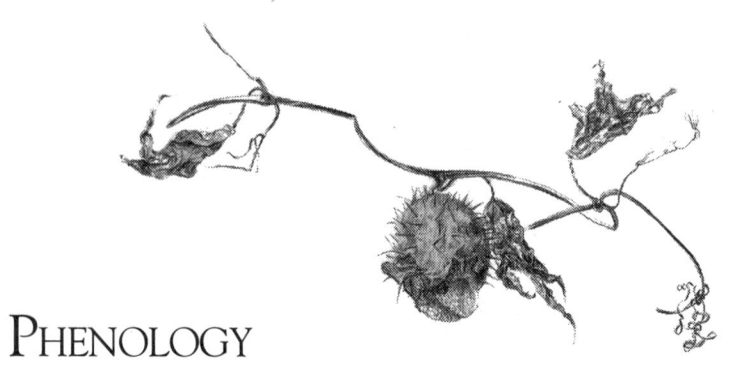

# PHENOLOGY

September offers proof that things aren't always what they seem to be in nature. That's what makes the out-of-doors so much fun.

Take birds, for instance. On early morning September walks you might hear more birds singing than you expect — the bright whistle of a cardinal, the distinctive phrasing of a migrating white-throated sparrow, or the spring song of a chickadee. Perhaps they're not in full voice as they are in May, but they're still the same songs that you looked forward to at the end of a long winter. Such fall singing occurs in several species, so September mornings can provide unanticipated music.

Another unexpected event is the sight of a white-tailed deer with bloody antlers and a blood smeared face. Our first reaction is one of fear that the animal is badly injured, but that's not the case. What has happened? The buck has been rubbing his antlers, probably on the trunk of a small tree, to remove the velvet that has covered his growing antlers since last spring. A few bucks start rubbing a little too early and break small blood vessels that remain in the velvet they are trying to shed. They may look gory, but they're not really hurt and they won't be bloody long. Buck whitetails usually have two antler-rubbing periods, one in early fall to clean off the velvet, and another in the late fall rutting season when they're thinking seriously about the opposite sex.

Plants also behave unexpectedly. Several species normally flowering in early spring sometimes produce a few plants that also will bloom in fall. For example, watch for the occasional blue violet that will flower briefly in September or October. Wild strawberries in bloom are another possibility.

This behavior seems to indicate that the physiology of plants is not quite as simple as we might think. It takes just the right combination of temperature, moisture, sunlight, darkness, soil nutrients and probably other factors to stimulate a particular plant to bloom out of its normal season. There can be many surprises in September, but most months are like that if you keep a sharp eye on your surroundings.

Don't overlook the wide variety of birdwatching possibilities this month offers. Early migrant flocks of ducks are found on lakes and marshes, especially blue-winged teal, wood duck and American wigeon. Small, loose flocks of broad-winged hawks, sometimes called "kettles," may be seen drifting slowly southward. Many shorebirds are still at peak migration numbers, among them dunlin, semipalmated sandpiper, solitary sandpiper, pectoral sandpiper and both species of yellowlegs.

Nighthawks may pass overhead in early evening hours. Their long, pointed wings with large white underwing patches make them easy to recognize. The wood warblers in their dull fall plumages and white-throated sparrows become abundant again, just as they were in late April and May. The first dark-eyed juncos and American tree sparrows arrive from the north, many of them to overwinter at our latitude.

Keep an eye skyward; there's a chance that a migrating flock of Canada geese or sandhill cranes can be spotted. You'll probably hear them before you see them.

Other signs of the approaching cold are white-tailed deer which are molting their red summer coats and growing brown winter pelage. Some in the middle of this change are quite bi-colored.

Look also for the older, inner needles on white and red pines to turn brown and begin to fall; this is a natural and annual drop that doesn't mean the trees are sick.

Even though a few tree leaves are beginning to turn color, the Arboretum is still bright with asters, goldenrods, and sunflowers. Weeds such as mullein, nightshade and Queen Anne's lace contribute blooms, but the incomparably blue gentians are the stars of the September flower show. Look for fringed, bottle, stiff and cream gentians in the moister sections of the prairies.

October offers variety. Hazy Indian summer days, frosty nights, or clear blue skies above the reds and yellows of fall foliage are only part of the picture.

While the oaks and maples are at their most brilliant, a few flowers are lingering. The last blooms of goldenrods, sunflowers, asters and gentians occupy the prairies. White snakeroot can be seen at the wood's edges. Weeds such as butter-and-eggs, yarrow, daisy fleabane and white campion continue in flower. Poison ivy is at its prettiest, showing dark red leaves and short stalks of shiny white berries. They're not recommended for table decorations, however.

Red-osier dogwood is a persistent bloomer; flowers and berries still might be found on the same bush. There are plenty of wild fruits and nuts to identify, among them mountain ash, bittersweet, nannyberry, black walnut, hazel and shagbark hickory.

Muskrats are building houses in the marshes around Lake Wingra. Squirrels and chipmunks are fattening on black and white oak acorns.

Birds are on the move. Peak numbers of migrant ducks, Canada geese, white-throated sparrows, pied-billed grebes, ruby-crowned kinglets and American coots, among others, should be in southern Wisconsin. Common loons reappear as migrants on Madison's lakes. Winter-resident birds such as evening gros-beaks, snow buntings and rough-legged hawks are arriving.

Most migratory songbirds have left us, but flocks of red-wings, robins and grackles are still using the marshes and woods. Rusty blackbirds might be seen in the Wingra Springs area.

Late in the month look for a sub-species of American robin with pale gray backs and gray-orange breasts; these birds with a faded-out look are a northern race that passes through but does not nest in Wisconsin.

Human phenology tells of seasonal changes, too. Mounds of raked-up leaves at the curb, gardens covered with motley collections of cloths and plastic on cold nights, vacant swimming beaches, and a switch to heavier clothing all point to colder weather. My favorite story along these lines came from an old-timer who predicted a hard winter because the neighbors put up their storm windows early.

November brings one of my favorite outdoor experiences — the passage of a migrating flock of tundra swans. Their mellow "woo-hoo" calls, often heard before the birds are seen, followed by a sighting of their wavering skein against a cold November sky provides a feeling of wildness that is seldom surpassed.

Field botanizing is more than flower-watching, so now, before heavy snows flatten many herbaceous plants, is a good time to practice identification skills on the Arboretum prairie. Many mature prairie plants have characteristic shapes and colors after the growing season.

The gold and wine-red tints of the fall prairies come mainly from the tall grasses. Two species of *Andropogon*, big and little bluestem, have a reddish cast. Big bluestem grows to a height of six feet or more and has three-branched clusters of flowers or seeds at the end of the stalks that accounts for its other name, turkeyfoot. Little bluestem is shorter and has feathery seed clusters which gives rise to its other name, beardgrass.

Indiangrass (*Sorghastrum*) is another six-footer with a prominent bushy seed head. Its color is more gold than red. Shorter grasses include side-oats grama (*Bouteloua*) with its seeds all on one side of its stem, and needle grass (*Stipa*) with inch-long needle-sharp seeds like porcupine quills.

Many other species are easy to spot. The tall stalks of the two *Silphium* species, prairie dock and compass plant, are topped by large round seed heads resembling small crowns. Prairie clover (*Petalostemum*) heads look like silver thimbles. Once the seeds of New Jersey tea (*Ceanothus*) fall, the remaining nickel-sized, flat-topped heads seem to be a group of tiny trumpets pointed at the sky. There are, of course, many more interesting species to identify. Give it a try.

November is the prelude to winter. While its days sometimes are bleak, even snowy, it is always an interesting time.

Wildflowers are nearly gone. A few late-blooming asters and goldenrods may persist in sheltered places. Canada goldenrod patches offer a bonus to ice fishermen — the stem galls contain a white grub that is an excellent panfish bait.

Look for a witch hazel bush or two in the Curtis Prairie parking lot along McCaffrey Drive. This medium-sized shrub is different in that it flowers after its leaves drop in the fall. Small yellow blossoms with narrow curly petals form when leaves are gone. Blooms persist well into November.

A number of woody plants should be retaining their fruits and adding color to the landscape: examples are mountain ash, highbush cranberry, winterberry, and the ornamental crab apples.

Any buck white-tailed deer you may see will be wearing its fully polished antlers. Deer sex identification is always easy in November.

Last but not least is the promise of cold to come. Lake Wingra usually freezes over in the fourth week of November.

# PLANTS, ANIMALS
# & OTHER THINGS IN SEASON

## AS THE LEAF TURNS ...

Invariably, every fall someone asks why tree leaves turn color. And usually, having not thought about this for some time, my definitely fallible memory does me in and I scurry to hunt up the notes from my course in beginning botany. But for this book, I have anticipated the question, so here is how it works.

There are five stars in this production. Remember their names, but don't let their complexity scare you off — abscission layer, chlorophyll, auxin, carotene and anthocyanin. Perhaps abscission layer is the most important, because our color show wouldn't happen without it.

All summer long, a tree's leaves produce food from air, water and soil nutrients which are circulated throughout the tree in a complicated system of minute tubes which make growth of the tree possible. Chlorophyll is the most visible food, because its green color is what we see in leaves during the growing season. Leaves also produce carotene and anthocyanin at the same time, but their colors are masked by the chlorophyll.

A fourth chemical, auxin, is produced in leaves and regulates our fifth actor in this drama, the abscission layer. This layer is a special band of cells at the base of each leaf stem which forms as leaves age. During the growing season, the auxin prevents the abscission layer from blocking the tubes that connect the leaf to the rest of the tree's circulatory system. In early fall, however, cooler and shorter days trigger an end to auxin production, which then allows the abscission layer to complete its growth and block off circulation to the leaves.

Now the tree's hidden colors come into view. Chlorophyll disintegrates rapidly, and the remaining chemicals have their day. The newly exposed carotene provides the yellow colors in maple, aspen and birch leaves. It's the same chemical that gives a yellow color to egg yolks and carrots.

The other previously hidden chemical, anthocyanin, provides the oranges and reds of maples, sumacs and oaks, as well as the purples of the ashes. If there are few sunny days, the anthocyanin will not be as chemically active and colors will be more orange or yellow than red.

The folklore about Jack Frost painting the leaves in full color is, unfortunately, not true. The most brilliant colors appear in periods when days are filled with bright sunshine, and nights are cool. Frost alone plays no part in the coloring of leaves, but if it is severe, might hasten the end of the autumn color period by causing leaves to fall early.


## BURNING QUESTIONS

Late fall is a season of reversals. A green landscape turns yellow, red and brown. Leafy trees become bare. Days are no longer warm. Rain is replaced by snow. How pleasant it is to sit by a crackling fireplace and watch the season's first snowfall. However, "pleasant" is a relative term. The kind of wood you are burning can influence the pleasure in your fire.

My dad kept a large wood box in our basement. Keeping it filled was a yearlong effort. He often came home lugging assorted wood to cut up for our fires. Tree limbs, old boards from a neighbor's remodeling project, scrap lumber from the local farm wagon factory, and wood pallets from the hardware store's junk pile all ended up in our wood box.

We burned a lot of wood in the winter and never had to pay for any of it. I'm still tempted to bring home scrap wood I see piled at the curb on trash pick-up days. However, most of us are burning wood that has not been turned into lumber, so it pays to know the characteristics of each species.

Hardwoods make the best fires, as they burn the longest and produce the most heat. Oak and hard maple are my favorites. Also in this category are hickory, birch, ash, locust, apple, elm, cherry and soft maple.

The softwoods are easy to light and provide medium heat, but they burn faster than hardwoods. This group includes the pines, cedar, fir, aspen, spruce, cottonwood and basswood. A good technique is to start a fire with softwood kindling and keep it going with hardwood chunks.

Perhaps the most obvious and important factor in fire building is to use only dry wood. Any freshly cut wood should be allowed to season in a dry place for six months to a year. If you can't store firewood under cover, a plastic tarp over the top of the woodpile will keep most of it dry all year.

Wood kept outdoors becomes a home for a variety of insects, so if you bring it indoors in winter, burn it right away so that several days in a warm place won't bring you unwanted guests revived by the heat.

# FALLING SEEDS

Fall is a well-named season. Many things are falling, among them night-time temperatures, acorns and other nuts, tree leaves, and apples.

Flower seeds also are falling. Not all of them simply fall by gravity as their pods dry and open. Jewelweed seeds are thrown sideways for several feet by the explosive splitting of their ripened seed capsules. Fluffy thistle and milkweed seeds are scattered by the wind. Burdocks, beggar-ticks and other burry types are pulled off their parent plants by a passing furred animal, or your jeans, or shoelaces, or worse yet, a child's hair.

Of all the falling plant life we see in October, acorns are among the most valuable to wild animals. Most mature oaks produce acorns. The four main species found in the Arboretum are the bur, white, red, and black oaks. They usually can be told apart by characteristics of their leaf shapes, bark, and acorns.

Acorns ripen and drop over several months. Bur oaks usually fall in August, white and red oaks in September, and black oaks in late September and October.

Acorns are palatable to many animals. They are a major fall food source for squirrels and white-tailed deer. Chipmunks, mice, common grackles, bluejays, and wild turkeys also favor acorns for food. Squirrels often begin feeding on acorns before they are ripe and will continue to hunt them on the ground, even burrowing into the snow to find them when winter comes. Deer seek out oak areas in winter and will paw up leaves to locate acorns until the snow becomes quite deep.

Acorns also are eaten by people. White oaks are the best. When roasted or boiled they have a rather bland nutty flavor. Other species of acorns are quite bitter due to the substantial amount of tannin they contain. If you want to try eating acorns, a little practice in oak identification should enable you to gather white oak acorns only.

## THE FINAL FLOWER OF FALL

If there is really a last rose of summer, then the final flower of fall surely must be an aster. Asters normally bloom from late July into October, with a few species persisting well past the first frosts into November. Among these late ones in the Madison area is the aptly named frost aster *(Aster pilosus)*.

Asters are members of the daisy family (Asteraceae). This is a very large group that includes goldenrods as well as all the daisy-like plants. Some botanists believe that the Asteraceae is the most recent plant family to appear on earth.

More than 60 species of asters are found in northeast and north-central North America. Most field guides don't list them all, but include 20 or so "representative" species.

This means that aster identification is difficult. The flower heads resemble miniature daisies in shape. Each has a button-like center of closely packed, minute disk flowers surrounded by a ring of flat, strap-shaped ray flowers — "rays" that look like petals. Individual species may occur in more than one color, ranging from white through pink to lavender and blue. They also may hybridize with one another, thereby adding confusion to identification. There are many leaf shapes, from broad to grasslike.

Identification is based on leaf form, diameter of the flower, color and number or rays. A few species, such as large-leaved (A. *macrophyllus),* New England (A. *novae-angliae)* and redstem (A. *puniceus),* are easy to spot, but by and large, positive identification may not be possible without resorting to highly technical characteristics not easily observed.

If you absolutely have to know which species is which, be prepared for a difficult time. I have found it much easier to settle for simply identifying them by color — white aster, blue aster, or purple aster.

One helpful aspect of asters is that their rays are never yellow. The disk flowers of many members of the daisy family, including asters, are sometimes orange or yellow, but if the rays are yellow, it isn't an aster.

Despite their abundance, asters are not a significant food source for birds and mammals. Rabbits and deer may browse a few leaves, and winter finches occasionally will eat aster seeds, but that's about it.

Our wild asters are the ancestors of the many cultivated asters so popular in summer flower gardens. Look for October's asters in open fields and woods edges, grassy wetlands and roadsides. They add much to the mid-fall landscape.

## The Fairies' Flowers

September is gentian month. These mostly bright blue, tubular flowers are the jewels of the prairie and well worth a hike to see. Five species of gentians from three genera should be found on the Greene Prairie during September.

The fringed gentian (*Gentianopsis crinita*) is perhaps the showiest. Growing up to three feet tall, its fringed petals flare out at the top of a deep tubular corolla. Individual blossoms grow on long stalks.

Downy gentians (*Gentiana puberula*) are shorter than two feet tall. They differ from their fringed cousins in that their petals are not fringed and they grow in a mostly stalkless cluster.

Bottle or closed gentians (*G. andrewsii*), as their name implies, have petals that stay closed and grow in stalkless clusters on one to two-foot stems.

Cream gentians (*G. flavida*) are shaped like bottle gentians with flowers of creamy white instead of blue.

Stiff gentians (*Gentianella quinquefolia*) are short — less than 18 inches — with tight clusters of small, tubular but open flowers which have bristle-pointed lobes. They are more lilac than blue in color, and tend to grow in groups of five per stem.

Gentians also have a place in folklore and folk medicine. As early as 200 B.C., a European gentian root was found to effectively treat malaria. When European colonists came to America, our native stiff gentian's roots were substituted for the European species, with success.

An old fairy tale says that some gentian blooms are always closed because once upon a time a group of fairies traveling in late summer were not allowed by a group of gentians to spend the night in their flowers. Ever after, those particular gentians were forced by the fairies to remain closed and keep their inner beauty hidden.

You will probably find more closed gentians than fairies on Greene Prairie, but who knows? And certainly, the gentians have their own magic!

# A GOOD WITCH NAMED HAZEL

On the west side of the Curtis Prairie parking lot on Arboretum Drive, you will find a surprise during early November — a tall, leafless, native shrub in flower. Its name is witch hazel (*Hamamelis virginiana*). I like it because of its odd growth habits and unusual uses.

Witch hazel blossoms have four curly yellow petals about one-half inch long. They do not appear until October and November after the oval, wavy-margined leaves have fallen. The fertilized flowers stay dormant until spring, when they develop into a capsule bearing a single hard seed.

Come fall, seed capsules explode when ripe and expel their seeds up to twenty feet. This can occur when the parent shrub is flowering, so you have the unusual situation of new flowers and mature seeds present on the same plant at the same time.

It is possible to be forcefully struck by a cast seed while you are looking at a blossom. (Artist Jane Bianco, while drawing a seed capsule in her studio, had just that experience. She recommends keeping any specimens under study in a glass jar, or wearing glasses.)

This seed-shooting habit led early people to believe that the plant was bewitched; hence its common name. The scientific name comes from two Greek words: *hama*, meaning "at the same time," and *melis*, meaning "a fruit."

Witch hazel extracts have been widely used as herbal medicine for hundreds of years. The liquid has alleged properties as an astringent, tonic, sedative and hemostat. It is claimed to relieve aching backs, sore muscles, diarrhea, dysentery and hemorrhoids. A snuff made of dried leaves is said to stop nosebleeds. The medicinal value of these uses is questionable.

Euell Gibbons wrote that "witch hazel will help nearly everything, but not very much." Even so, it is still a popular product sold in drug stores, for use as the equivalent of rubbing alcohol.

Leaving folk medicine, another offbeat use for this plant can be found in folk science. A forked witch hazel branch makes a highly favored divining rod for dowsing underground water and metals.

Among all these putative powers and cures, the shrub offers one certain danger. If you stand close to a November witch hazel, you should beware of flying seeds.


## GOLDENROD GALLS

Bright yellow patches of Canada goldenrod are a common and beautiful feature of the late summer and fall landscape. Their robust stalks also persist through the winter as easily recognized three-foot brown stems topped by a pyramidal gray plume of seed heads.

Goldenrod plants aren't just visually attractive. They also serve as hosts to invertebrate animals. Young spiders, for example, often spend the winter in a silky nest within the plumed tops.

A conspicuous round gall on many goldenrod stems is the home of an insect called, logically enough, the round goldenrod gall fly. These galls are often abundant in many stands of Canada goldenrod and are easy to see against the snow.

The adult gall fly is about the size of a house fly, but has brown wings with white spots. The flies in summer insert their eggs singly into the goldenrod stem and the plant grows the gall around the egg. Galls seem to have little effect on the vigor of the host plant. After hatching, the larva stays inside the gall, using it both as food and winter protection. The adult fly emerges from the gall in spring and the life cycle begins again.

The larvae are of some use as a popular panfish bait for ice fishing. Galls can be collected and stored in a cold place until they are to be used for this purpose. However, warm storage will cause the larvae to pupate and thus be of no use for fishing.

If you'd like a good look at the adult fly, keep a gall or two in a glass jar with a ventilated top in a warm room for two or three weeks. Lightly sprinkle the galls with water once a week to simulate outdoor spring conditions and soon the adult fly will emerge.

A second species of stem gall is also found on Canada goldenrod, this one caused by the solidago gall moth. This is a small moth named for the Latin name of the goldenrod genus, *Solidago*. Its gall is spindle-shaped, not round. You won't find larvae over-wintering in these galls because the eggs hatch and mature to adult form during the spring and summer. Eggs are then laid on goldenrod stems in the fall, and do not hatch until the following spring.

You may find galls that have been eaten into. Such damage is usually done by downy woodpeckers, a bird with fondness for the gall larvae. If you're after fish bait, the birds may have beaten you to it.

# WETLAND MONARCH

Early October is a good time to get acquainted with a tamarack (*Larix laricina*), which just happens to be my favorite Wisconsin tree. Tamaracks are the only conifers native to Wisconsin that shed all their needles in the fall and grow a complete new set each spring. In late September and October the needles turn a shade of yellow that Aldo Leopold described as "smoky gold." By November, the needles usually are gone.

Tamaracks are a wetland tree. They thrive in wet soils and can grow to a height of 50 feet or more. They don't do well in standing water. Their root systems are shallow, seldom deeper than 18 inches, but may spread to a width greater than the height of the tree. Seedlings require full sunlight and will not grow in the shade of the parent trees.

Tamarack needles are short and grow in clusters of about 20. They are a pleasant gray-green in color and quite soft to the touch. In spring, as the new needles are emerging, bright pink cones appear on the outer branches, creating an appearance much different from their fall gold. Ripe cones are brown and about three-fourths of an inch long.

There are a few large tamaracks in the Arboretum's East Marsh. Tamaracks at Big Spring are more easily seen. The tamaracks you see in urban landscape plantings most likely are one of several Old-World species commonly called larch.

Tamaracks do have problems. They are very susceptible to ground fires and to an insect pest, the larch sawfly. Many stands in southern Wisconsin have been decimated by these two agents.

I first got close to tamaracks about 50 years ago when the other Arboretum biologists and I made a midsummer trip to a Waukesha County tamarack swamp. We went there to cut poles for building a bird-watching blind in the West Marsh.

Tamarack wood is very dense, heavy and water-resistant, making it ideal for use in damp situations. While in the swamp I was impressed by the rather stately aspect of the trees, the gentle texture of their needles and their soft gray-green appearance. I also became acquainted with a less pleasing species, poison sumac, which provided me with a blistered arm before the day was over.

I later learned that tamaracks keep company with more friendly species such as bottle gentians, Labrador tea, Canada mayflower, ladyslippers and other wild orchids, ruffed grouse and woodcock. Deer also spend time among the tamaracks, especially when they want heavy cover for protection from winter storms and cold.

Watch for October tamaracks glowing against a backdrop of pines or firs. It can be a spectacular scene.

# THE UPS AND DOWNS OF MIGRATION

The seasonal travels of animals that we call migration can take many forms. Barn swallows make annual round trip flights from Canada to South America. Deer mice may move from the woods to your garage in fall. Little brown bats travel many miles to the caves where they will hibernate over winter. Monarch butterflies may fly to Mexico.

Such movements may be described as horizontal migrations because they take place, for the most part, above ground. But great numbers of small, lesser-known animals also have fall and spring migrations that are vertical, not horizontal.

With the onset of cold days, insects, spiders, snails, mites and other small invertebrate creatures creep downward from tall grasses, shrubs and trees to the ground cover. Some will stay in the leaf mold all winter and some will burrow into the soil. Many species don't go below the soil surface because they can survive being frozen over winter.

Other animals work their way into the soil. Earthworms and May beetles may dig down several feet to stay below the frost zone. Even larger forms such as toads dig into the soil until spring.

Amphibians, including leopard frogs and tiger salamanders, move from the woods and marshes to join turtles for the winter under rocks or in the mud at the bottoms of ponds and streams. Most aquatic animals, including fish and insects, move from shallow water to deep water during the cold season.

Hibernating mammals such as chipmunks, spermophiles and woodchucks spend their winter in underground burrows.

# THAT MOUSE IN YOUR HOUSE

It all started toward the end of August. I went into our garage one morning and noticed a small pile of chewed-up plastic gasket from the bottom of the garage door. The pile was guarding a small hole to the outside.

Well, I thought, they're back, but maybe they left again through this hole. The next morning my entry to the garage was greeted by strenuous rustlings behind the woodpile. This time I knew it was serious. The annual pre-winter invasion of mice was under way.

Whether you live in the city, in the suburbs or in the country, you can expect this problem. Anytime from mid-summer to the first heavy snows, a mouse (or two) is apt to join you for the winter. Attached garages and basements are their favorites residences; after all, where better to find warmth, cover and food?

Once mice find you, and vice versa, there is only one way to meet the problem successfully, short of adopting several house cats, and that is a couple of old fashioned snap traps baited with peanut butter. In our case, one trap caught two mice in three days and temporarily cleaned them out of the garage.

Rodent poisons are available, but poisoned mice have a habit of dying in places where you can smell them but not find them. Of course, if you can't bear to run a trap line for mice, a supply of sunflower seeds and cracked corn will keep them happy all winter.

There are two species of people-friendly mice common in southern Wisconsin. The closer you live to the center of town, the more apt your resident rodent will be a house mouse (*Mus musculus*). This is an Old-World species well established in North America since colonial days. It is six to seven inches long, dark brownish gray above and pale gray below, with a nearly hairless tail as long as its head and body. The ears are large and the eyes are bright. House mice set up housekeeping almost anyplace in a building where they are not disturbed.

If you're a suburbanite or rural resident, you might acquire a house mouse, but more likely you'll get a deer mouse (*Peromyscus*). As mice go, deer mice (sometimes called white-footed mice) are beauties. They are gray brown with white feet and underbody. About the same size as a house mouse, their hairy tails are usually bicolored and are slightly shorter than their bodies. Their ears and eyes are large. Several species of deer mouse are native to Wisconsin.

# THE HOMELY DIGGERS

If there ever is a contest for Wisconsin's homeliest mammal, the common mole should be a top contender. This mole, often called prairie mole, is an Arboretum resident and is widely distributed in areas of light soil in southern and western Wisconsin.

The only other mole species in the state is confined to northern counties. It is the star-nosed mole, also a potential non-beauty winner, and is so named because it has a circle of 22 fleshy tentacles around its nose which apparently serve as sense organs during underground travel.

The name "mole" is derived from an old English word "mould-warp", meaning an animal that warps or throws up the mold or soil. Both mole species spend most of their lives underground digging tunnels and burrows, so their name is fitting.

The common mole usually is found in sandy soils and light loams, pastures, cultivated fields, gardens, lawns and woodlands. Moles can be detected by the ridges of earth they throw up while they are burrowing just under the surface. The sandy trails around the Greene Prairie area are good places to spot mole tunnels in the Arboretum. These tunnels can be harmful to lawns, gardens and golf courses, but where they are not a problem, the diggings are helpful in aerating soil and accelerating surface water absorption.

Common moles are about the size of a small rat (7 to 8 inches long, including a short tail) with a sharply pointed muzzle, tiny weak eyes and dense, dark gray-brown fur. Their most notable features are their muscular front legs, which are adapted for digging. The front paws are much broader than long, and bear wide, flat claws. The palms face outward. They are very efficient burrowers.

In late fall, moles still dig, but deeper in the earth to stay below the frost line. They do not hibernate and may be active at any time of the day or night.

Insects, earthworms, and other invertebrate animals make

up about 85 percent of their diet. They are voracious eaters and have been observed to eat their own weight in food in a 24-hour period. They will on occasion eat grass, corn and fruit.

If you live all your life underground, I guess it doesn't matter if you're beautiful or not.

## BIRD MIGRATIONS

When many of the birds you see in September seem to belong in the "confusing fall warblers" section of your field guide, you know that the annual fall migration is on. Goldfinches, bobolinks, indigo buntings, terns, starlings, and many of the ducks and shorebirds, as well as warblers and other species, molt their feathers into a fall and winter plumage that differs from the one they wear in spring. In addition, the young of many species have dull first-year plumages that are quite different from their adult colors.

Thus the birdwatcher's life is more complicated in fall. That strange-looking bird you see this month may be just one of your old friends from last spring in a new coat of feathers.

Bird migrations have fascinated people for centuries. More than 2,000 years ago, Aristotle proclaimed that birds disappeared in fall because they found hiding places and hibernated until spring. Other writers believed that swallows spent the winter in the mud of marshes.

Several books in the Bible refer to migrations. The author of Jeremiah , for example, wrote, "Even storks know when it is time to return; doves, swallows and thrushes know when it is time to migrate.(8:7)"

We have come a long way from the days when hummingbirds were said to travel on the backs of Canada geese. Centuries of study, plus modern technology, have shown bird migration to involve complicated relationships between day length, weather, magnetic fields, endocrine interactions, fat deposition, and physiological conditioning, but how these

84

and other factors operate to regulate migratory behavior is not completely understood.

Even though scientists are still searching for more whys and hows, nothing prevents those of us who watch birds from learning to know what we see at the far end of our binoculars in the fall season. Like golf or bowling, fall birding takes lots of practice, but such practice can be a lot of fun.

# THE BIRDS OF FALL

It may be September, but it isn't time to put away your binoculars for the year. Late summer and early fall can provide a good deal of excellent birding if you're willing to be patient and search out the more productive habitats.

For example, check the edges of wetland ponds. This is the time when the young of several herons begin to wander from their home areas and are apt to be seen in any part of southern Wisconsin. Great egrets, cattle egrets, snowy egrets, and the all-white juvenile little blue herons are possibilities.

Other species of water birds also may be increasing in marshes with open water. Early migrant flocks of blue-winged teal and American widgeon lead the southward parade of other ducks. Pied-billed grebes and American coots should become more numerous, while shorebirds such as semipalmated sandpipers, dunlins, and common snipe are also migrating.

Don't ignore the wandering flocks of ring-billed and herring gulls. They may have a Caspian tern among them. Caspians are the size and color of herring gulls, but lack black wing tips, and have mostly black caps and bright orange bills.

An eye on the sky might locate loose congregations of migrating broad-winged hawks. If you're lucky, you might spot a few nighthawks overhead also, but their numbers have declined in recent years and they're no longer abundant.

It might help to keep your ears open, too. At this time of year, cock ring-necked pheasants will crow and male ruffed grouse will perform on their drumming logs just as they do in spring. It's usually the birds hatched last summer, rather than older males, that sound off in fall, something like a practice session for next spring.

You may find hundreds of tree and barn swallows lined up on rural telephone wires. Such spectacular flocks gather just before they migrate south; so they won't remain long in the same area.

White-throated sparrows become more numerous in our area during September. Most of them are heading south. Another early migrant is the rusty blackbird, which has a preference for shrubby wetlands such as the Arboretum's Wingra Springs.

# House Cleaning — It's for the Birds

Wildflowers are gone for the year, leaves are mostly down, and only the winter birds will be with us for a while, so now is a good time to do some fall house cleaning — bird-house cleaning, that is. All bird houses that birds aren't using as a night roosting place will last longer and be more attractive to next year's residents if they are cleaned out and taken inside over winter.

This cleaning-up process even can be educational. Sometimes nest materials and how birds use them are surprising. House wrens are a good case in point.

University of Wisconsin-Madison Professor Robert McCabe studied the components of 52 wren nests, built at the Arboretum in three-quart tin cans adapted for nest boxes. Wren nests are built in two stages. The first, made by the male, is a bulky mass of twigs with a nest depression in the rear of the box opposite the entrance.

Honeysuckle, black cherry and oak twigs headed the list of 36 plant species used in male nests. In any one nest, one species usually made up about two-thirds of the weight of the nest. The frequency of plant species use corresponded to the abundance of that plant near the nest site.

Males that found mates early in the season built smaller nests than males that did not mate until later. Unsuccessful males frequently filled the entire nest can with twigs.

The second stage, the lining of the nest cavity prior to egg laying, is done only by the female. Feathers representing 25 bird species, grass, spider egg-sac cotton, pine needles, snake skin fragments, other small plant parts, and horse hair were most often used for lining. Cellophane cigar wrappers, twine, and bits of thin transparent plastic were sometimes found in nests.

McCabe commented, "If cigar wrappers can replace snake skins, twine can replace horse hair, and metal can replace wood, we need not fear for the survival of the house wren in man's synthetic environment."

## ARACHNID SPINNERS AND WEAVERS

To most people, spiders rank right up there in unpleasantness along with snakes, bats, skunks and mosquitos. But as is the case with all such species, spiders are not nearly as bad as you might think.

Spiders are not insects. They are in a group of animals called Arachnids, which also includes mites, scorpions and harvestmen (or daddy-long-legs). Spiders have eight legs; insects have only six.

Spiders are ancient creatures; they are believed to be at least 400 million years old and were among the first animals that learned to live on land.

There are several hundred species of spiders in the United States, and they come in many sizes and colors. They can be found most anywhere, from basements to the treetops.

Spiders eat mainly insects. Since beneficial as well as harmful insects are preyed upon indiscriminately, people are rather neutral as to their usefulness.

Spiders do not bite unless they are held or squeezed. The bites of only the very large tropical species are virulent enough to seriously affect humans. Our Wisconsin spiders do not carry diseases.

Spiders are most noted for building webs to trap their prey. Their webs vary in design between species. Some are architecturally marvelous structures suspended from vegetation; they often become subjects for photographers. Others are shaped more like cocoons or sheets, but their purposes are the same — to catch a meal. The silk with which spiders spin webs comes from several specialized organs on their bodies called spinnerets.

Spiders would seem to be sedentary, but some are capable of traveling many miles — by air. In late summer and fall, many newly hatched spiders will climb to the top of any handy vegetation on a breezy day and begin to spin a strand of silk. These strands are light enough and strong enough to be carried by the wind, and when they become long enough will pick up the spinner and carry it along until some object is contacted.

Such small "ballooning" spiders sometimes can be seen from the deck of the McKay Center on late fall afternoons.

WINTER

# PHENOLOGY

$D$ecember may find us grumbling about the cold days, and the land may be buried in snow, but the orderly progressions of natural events we study as phenology are proceeding as usual. Some of them we can see; others are only heard. For example, listen on cold, calm winter nights near the woods for the calls of great horned owls announcing their territory in preparation for egg-laying and incubation in February.

Insects overwinter in a variety of forms. Look for the large fuzzy cocoons of cecropia moths attached lengthwise to the twigs of shrubs or low trees. They will produce the next generation of moths come warm weather. Another over-wintering form waiting for spring is the belt of tent-caterpillar moth eggs found on twigs of apple and wild cherry trees.

Our early-spring butterfly, the mourning cloak, hibernates in its adult form in any convenient shelter, even in buildings. And some of the yellow jacket wasps that pestered last fall will return after they have spent the winter in old stumps, rotten logs, under buildings or in brush piles.

While many well-known mammals hibernate (such as chipmunk, spermophile, woodchuck, little brown bat), others are active the year around and will begin breeding or are in their gestation period in mid-winter. For example, red foxes, mink, and gray squirrels will start mating in late January, while white-tailed deer and long-tailed weasels carry their young all winter following their fall breeding seasons.

January is a good time to look for birds that visit southern Wisconsin only in winter. Most of the birds are sparrow-sized members of the finch family, but a few larger songbirds and raptors are usually present, too.

Look for snow buntings and lapland longspurs, often in large flocks, on prairies, open fields and airports. Roughlegged hawks, including their attractive black color phase, and snowy owls also may be seen in these habitats. The owls sometimes are found in marshes and on frozen lakes.

Open woods, woods edges, roadsides, brushy and weedy fields, and bird feeders are good places to find northern juncos, tree sparrows, common and hoary redpolls (the hoary is rare), pine siskins and northern shrikes (another rarity). Siskins often hang out with goldfinches at feeders.

Stands of pine, spruce and fir may hold white-winged crossbills and red crossbills (rare). Also in conifers, or in mixed woods and around feeders or fruiting trees and shrubs (apple, box elder, highbush cranberry, etc.), look for robin-sized evening grosbeaks, pine grosbeaks and bohemian waxwings. Goshawks are sometimes found in wooded areas.

All of these birds, except juncos and tree sparrows, are irregular visitors. In some winters they're abundant and in some they're scarce, depending on weather patterns, food supplies and other unknown factors.

*F*ebruary is a month of beginnings. Many of our resident birds are beginning to pair off and sing courtship songs, among them northern cardinals, black-capped chickadees, European starlings and mourning doves. The beaks of starlings are turning yellow and their plumage is becoming iridescent, signs that the nesting season is not far off. A few early migrant birds can also be seen, such as common goldeneye ducks, horned larks and red-winged blackbirds. Striped skunks and opossums are resuming their nightly wanderings. Look for their tracks in the snow.

Trees and shrubs can provide some interesting winter botanizing if you're willing to study them. Most woody plants in winter can be identified by their twigs and buds.

For example, a taste test will help determine several species. Juneberry (*Amelanchier*) twigs have an almond taste to go along with their long, sharply pointed buds that curve in towards the stem. Saplings of yellow birch (*Betula lutea*) and white birch (*B. papyifera*) look alike, but the yellow twigs taste like wintergreen while the white's flavor is very bitter. Choke cherry (*Prunus virginiana*) has buds that are conical, pointed and green in color plus an inner bark that has a disagreeable odor, while black cherry (*P. serotina*) has heart-shaped, fuzzy buds, with a yellowish color and an inner bark that is aromatic.

Learning which tree or shrub is which is not only interesting in itself, it also tells you what woody plants are being browsed by deer or barked and pruned by rabbits and mice in mid-winter.

And perhaps best of all, sunsets are getting later every day.

# Plants, Animals
# & Other Things in Season

## A Long Winter's Nap

As the nights grow longer and colder, early snows fall, and winter is just ahead, an interesting event is going on in the animal world.

It's called hibernation. Hibernation, put simply, is the state of becoming dormant over winter. A hibernator has low body temperature, reduced metabolic rates, no food intake, and sleeps for several months. A long winter's nap, indeed.

There is little pattern in who hibernates and who doesn't. One of Wisconsin's largest mammals, the black bear, hibernates — our smallest mammals, the shrews, do not. Jumping mice do, but deer mice and meadow voles do not. Chipmunks and 13-lined ground squirrels (often called spermophiles or gophers) do, but red and gray squirrels do not. Some kinds of bats do; others don't.

Many insect species do and many do not. Among butterflies, for example, mourning cloaks hibernate, but monarchs fly south for the winter. None of our birds are hibernators, but all our frogs, toads, salamanders, snakes and turtles hibernate — many of them underwater. No one seems to have found a reason why there is so much variation among hibernators, or how they developed the habit in the first place.

Zoologists tend to quibble about when slowed-down activity becomes true hibernation. Once a woodchuck, a true hibernator, nods off in its winter burrow, it sleeps there until spring. Raccoons and skunks will sleep for long periods, but a warm winter day may bring them out for a sluggish walk before they go back to bed. Are they really hibernating or not?

Most animals that are active all winter may lie low during bad weather, but this is not hibernation; it's just a temporary means of conserving body heat and energy.

Hibernating mammals go through remarkable physiological changes. Studies have shown that a 13-lined ground squirrel, for example, in summer breathes about 200 times per minute, has a heart beat of 300 times per minute, and a body temperature of about 95° Fahrenheit. While hibernating, however, it may breathe once or twice a minute, have a heart beat of five times per minute, and a body temperature nearly as low as the air surrounding it.

Most hibernating animals feed heavily in late summer and fall to lay on the body fat they will need to utilize through the winter.

There is another type of dormancy called estivation. This is the summer equivalent of hibernation. It is found among several kinds of invertebrate animals. When ponds occupied by caddis fly larvae dry up in mid summer, the larvae burrow into the mud of the pond bottom and stay there until the pond again fills with water. When certain snails are exposed to hot, dry conditions, they withdraw into their shells and cease all activity until more moisture is available.

I can identify with hibernators. Many times I would have preferred to stay under the nice warm blankets and not get up to shovel snow.

# WHERE HAVE ALL THE TURTLES GONE?

If you were a turtle, where would you spend the winter? Not all turtles are alike, so it depends on your species. However, all turtles do hibernate, so that answers part of the question; you'll stay close to where you spent the summer.

Take painted turtles (*Chrysemys picta*) for example, the most widely distributed species in Wisconsin. They're often seen in lakes, slow-moving streams and marshes, and are prone to being run over by cars on roads near their habitats.

Like the other turtles, painted turtles turn sluggish when temperatures drop below 60 degrees, and begin hibernation when it gets below freezing. Our painted turtles combat cold simply by digging into the mud at the bottom of their ponds or marshes and remaining there until spring warms the water.

Many painted turtles have two clutches of eggs per year, and those that hatch in late summer often spend the winter in the underground nest where they were born. The reasons why young turtles do this and how they can survive sub-zero temperatures while less than a foot below ground-level are unknown.

All turtles breathe air, so those species that spend the winter in the water have special adaptations. Their winter metabolism is much reduced and their need for oxygen is not large, but they still must breathe under water. On each side of their urinary bladder is an accessory bladder which can be filled and emptied with water. These bladders have many blood vessels which permit absorption of enough oxygen to keep the turtle alive.

Other Wisconsin turtles that winter under water include snapping, Blanding's, wood, softshell, map and false map. Snapping turtles hibernate in muskrat tunnels, holes in stream banks and in springs, as well as in lake and marsh bottoms. One Wisconsin turtle hibernates in burrows on dry land. This is the ornate box turtle. It digs a burrow in light soil that may be up two feet deep. Since it can continue to breathe air all winter, it does not have the special anatomical structures for oxygen transfer found in underwater hibernators. So if you are a turtle, you go down, not south, for the cold season.

## A WALK IN THE WOODS

When we leave the warmth of our beds on a February morning and peer out the window only to see a snow-covered, sub-zero world, it's easy to think that no living things are about. Hibernators are in deep sleep, migrants have all gone south, and no green leaves are in sight. But perhaps we have leaped to the wrong conclusion. A walk in the wood could produce surprises.

One of my mid-winter junkets did just that. It was a cloudless morning that belied a bitter cold brought by arctic winds. Sunlight on the snowbound earth provided a clarity of view marred only by the vapor cloud my breath cast out. The woods had a brilliance and a feeling of brittleness no other time of year provides. I brushed the snow from a fallen log and sat to watch.

A red squirrel, perched somewhere in a nearby pine, belabored me with loud abuse for trespass. Its gray squirrel cousin jumped in stately arcs across the snow, pausing to burrow in a drift with hopes for one more acorn.

Two raucous bluejays flew by, in search of who knows what, with frequent cries to tell the world they're here, and a tiny shrew emerged from an elderly stump, its twitching nose the symbol of a ceaseless search to fuel its boundless energy. Four crows passed overhead, soundless shadows in the sky, bound for some far cornfield. Chickadees, engaged in constant conversation and a never-ending hunt for food, left a residue of cheerfulness.

Dry, hanging oak leaves rustled as their branches creaked a protest to the wind, giving notice that their turn will come in spring, and the many tracks of white-tailed deer told me that their herd had passed this way last night.

We must conclude that our winter world is far from dead, even though we are only fragile islands in a sea of frozen air.

# LIFE BENEATH THE SNOW

Winter is no time for flower watching. The snow lies deep and the air is cold. The land remains beautiful, but how we would appreciate a glimpse of the first hepatica or a prairie in full summer bloom!

However, beneath the snow and the litter of dead leaves lies the promise of another season. The annual biological clock is ticking away as usual, and the roots of plants to come are in place. Roots are the key here. Seldom seen, under-appreciated, and hardly ever identified by the average flower watcher, roots are the source of all the colors of the growing season.

Roots come in all shapes and sizes — long, short, stringy, smooth, contorted, fleshy, round, tapered and so on. In general, perennial plants have larger and stronger roots than annuals, because perennials must store enough food over winter to provide for growth next spring.

Many plants, like Solomon's seal and bloodroot, are named for the characteristics of their roots. Other examples are redroot (or New Jersey tea), colic root, white snakeroot, Culver's root and cancer root.

Roots have three purposes: feeding the plant parts that grow above ground, supporting the growing stems and storing food for the future. Annual plants (those that grow and die in one year) do not store food in their roots and reproduce each year only from seed.

Some roots are useful as food, such as yams, carrots, beets, turnips, horseradish and chicory. Native Americans and the white pioneers found roots to be a source of dyes for fabrics, among them bloodroot for red and black walnut for black.

The early herbalists believed roots to be valuable in many ways. Gentian roots could cure malaria. Seneca snakeroot could cure snakebite. Solomon's seal has long rootstocks with scars where stems of past growing seasons have fallen away. These scars are the source of the plant's name. When cut transversely, they seemed to show King Solomon's seal, the six-pointed star.

Because of this, the crushed rootstocks became widely used to seal open wounds and mend broken bones.

Folklore is full of the power of roots. Queen Anne's lace roots placed under your pillow will make any of your dreams, good or bad, come true. But if you eat violet roots just before going to bed, your dreams will be pleasant and the Queen Anne's lace will make them come true.

Or how about a potato? If it's dried in the morning sun, but kept from the afternoon sun and carried on your person it will prevent arthritis. Whatever you do, don't transplant a lily of the valley or you will die within a year. Sprites guard the roots and train them to grown in special shapes. If you disrupt their growth by removing a plant, the sprites' work must be done over, and they will wreak revenge on the transplanter.

There is indeed much going on under the snow.


## THEY'RE STUCK ON YOU

The wildflowers are gone. Snow already has fallen. Trees and shrubs are bare. It's winter, but even though the landscape seems lifeless, things of interest can be seen.

Flowers are followed by seeds. Many of them are "burs" or "stick-tights." This is a good time to find and identify them. Walk through a woods, or a prairie, or a weedy field — if you're wearing any kind if rough-surfaced clothing, you will collect specimens.

If it has all-over prickly brown spines in a round ball the size of a Concord grape, you've snagged a burdock. If it's flat, roughly triangular, brown-black, about one-quarter inch long, with two barbed "legs" on the short side, you've found a beggar-tick. If it's three-quarters inch long, needle-like, black, slightly curved, with sharply pointed ends, you have acquired sweet cicely. If it's flat, feels sticky, and looks like a miniature segmented pea-pod, you have a tick-trefoil.

The largest of this group is common burdock, a member of the daisy family which produces a prickly, round bur. The bur forms under a small lavender flower and is composed of many bracts, each ending in a sharp hook. They stick easily to fur, feathers or wool jackets.

Burdock grows from one and one-half to five feet tall, usually on disturbed ground in either sun or shade. A circle of very large heart-shaped leaves surround the base of the plant. Its single flower stalk has much smaller leaves. This is an alien species introduced from Europe, and is well-established over much of the United States.

Despite its weedy reputation, burdock has some interesting characteristics. Its roots are edible if they are from first-year plants (burdock is a biennial), peeled, sliced and boiled or fried. Older roots are very bitter. Cooked roots may have a laxative effect if eaten in quantity. Domesticated burdock roots are grown in Japan and Hawaii, where they are a popular food known as gobo.

Burdock also has a place in herbal medicine. The raw juice from leaves, roots and stems has been used to treat eczema, burns and sores. An elixir from roots was formerly a common remedy for many ills, especially rheumatism. Roots are said to be rich in inulin, a starchy compound that converts to fruit sugar in water.

Wildlife makes some use of burdock seeds as food. In the late 1940s, when 200 or more ring-necked pheasants wintered in the Arboretum, it was common to find torn-up burs and pheasant tracks around burdock clumps.

A different use of burdock was made by my friends when I was in grade school. Someone discovered that a piece of burdock leaf made a good wrapper for our experimental corn-silk cigarettes. It was a fad that didn't last.

# THE GREENS OF WINTER

One pleasant part of winter botany is that our native pine trees are just as easy to identify now as they are in the growing season. Pines are coniferous (cone-bearing) trees that bear needle-like leaves which stay on the tree for several years.

Wisconsin has three native pines, all of which can be found in the Arboretum — eastern white (*Pinus strobus*), Norway or red (*P. resinosa*) and jack (*P. banksiana*). They can be told apart by the characters of their needles, cones and bark. (There are many other non-native pines used for ornamental purposes. Longenecker Gardens has a selection of such species.)

White pine needles grow in bundles of five that are three to five inches long, soft to the touch, and remain on the tree three to five years. The bark is smooth and greenish gray on young wood, but becomes thick, ridged and gray-black on the trunks of mature trees. Cones are five to ten inches long and slightly curved.

Norway pines have four- to six-inch, sharp-pointed needles in bundles of two which are partly covered by a membranous sheath. The needles do not fall until they are four or five years old. The bark is scaly with a reddish cast. Cones are about two inches long, stalkless, and rounded in shape.

Jack pines have flat, short (up to two inches) needles which grow in pairs and stay in place for two to three years. The cones are about as long as the needles and have a slightly bent, rounded form. The bark is dull brown and narrowly ridged.

A fourth species, scotch pine (P. sylvestris), is often grown for Christmas trees. It is perhaps the most popular species for this purpose. However, it is a native of northern Europe, not of Wisconsin. Its needles are shorter than those of Norway pine but longer than jack pine, and grow in two-needle bundles. The bark has a reddish cast. These pines seldom grow straight and tall in Wisconsin, so crooked trunks on Christmas trees are sometimes a problem.

Pines are not the only coniferous trees native to our state. There are five others that have short needles (eastern hemlock, black spruce, white spruce, tamarack, balsam fir) and two with scale-like leaves (northern white cedar, eastern red cedar or juniper). Tamaracks are different from the others in that they shed all their needles every year and are bare-branched all winter. The scaly leaves of cedars don't fall for several years.

# CITY CRITTERS

The growing season is gone and the winter bird-feeding season is upon us, and that has led me to ponder the status of urban birds in the Madison area.

What started this is the large increase in recent years of house finches at my feeders and an accompanying decline in house (or English) sparrows. I know of no cause-and-effect relationship between these two, but such changes in the bird world seem to be going on around us constantly.

Most people tend to view the outdoors as unchanging. If you have found wild geraniums in the Arboretum woods for several years, you assume that they will be there forever. Similar assumptions occur for such trees as white birch and aspen — and for backyard birds. But this is a shortsighted view; the natural world is dynamic, not static. Plant successions, weather trends, and periodic fluctuations in food supplies can cause changes in species compositions in any given year. Today's pasque flowers can be tomorrow's memories.

The same is true for our birds. Think about American crows in the city as far back as you can remember, and I hope you see the change. Madison is infested with urban crows citywide — a relatively recent development. House finches have exploded all over Wisconsin in the last decade. More mourning doves are wintering over in southern Wisconsin than did so several years back. More Cooper's and sharp-shinned hawks are patrolling our bird feeders. Fewer starlings haunt my feeders. Ring-necked pheasants have practically disappeared from the Arboretum.

Among the mammals, raccoons have adapted to city life, living in tree cavities, under sheds and in storm sewers, to say nothing of raiding home gardens and bird feeders — and Madison's resident white-tailed deer don't seem to be decreasing in numbers. But have you seen many Franklin's ground squirrels in the Arboretum lately? They used to be regular residents.

What did we do or not do to cause these changes? Is it because of us or in spite of us? I don't know, but it is a fascinating scene to watch. It gives me a good deal of comfort to realize that the human race has not achieved complete control over all the world's organisms, and that there are natural processes going on out there that don't need our help.


## FABULOUS FEATHERS

It's 6 degrees below zero outside my window and the wind chill is minus 30° Fahrenheit, but three chickadees are eating sunflower seeds as usual at the bird feeder. They seem oblivious to the cold; how do they manage to survive? The answer should be obvious — feathers.

On a day like this, all birds look fatter than usual because they have fluffed up their feathers to hold heat against their bodies. Insulation against extreme temperatures, both cold and hot, is just one function of feathers.

Depending on their species, feathers also enable birds to fly, to provide protective coloration against predators, to identify their species, to line their nests while incubating eggs, and to keep their bodies dry. (You very seldom see a wet duck.)

Birds are the only animals that have feathers. The number of feathers per bird may be as few as 1,500 on a hummingbird and as many as 25,000 on a tundra swan. All these feathers are molted periodically, sometimes twice a year, and replaced in a matter of weeks.

Water birds such as ducks and geese shed so many wing feathers at one time that they are flightless until replacements are grown. On the other hand, swallows which must feed in flight lose one matching wing feather at a time from each side so they can keep flying.

Birds have several varieties of feathers. Wings and tails have stiff central shafts. Growing from each side of this shaft are parallel branches called barbs. Each barb is edged with hooked branchlets called barbules. A barbule hooks itself to the barbule of the adjoining barb, thereby keeping the shape of the feather intact in the manner of a zipper. When you see a bird preening its feathers, it is running a feather through its bill and zipping the barbs together.

Some birds, such as kingfishers and woodpeckers, are born naked, but most others have at least a few short, fluffy, down feathers. Down is one of several specialized feather types. As young birds mature, the insulating down becomes covered with adult contour feathers which give the bird's body a characteristic shape. Contour feathers do not have the stiff central shaft of wing or tail feathers.

Scattered among the contour feathers, most birds have hair-like feathers called filoplumes. If you have ever plucked a chicken, these are the "hairs" that are left after you remove the larger feathers. Filoplumes are believed to have nerve endings at their bases which are sensors of environmental conditions and stimulate muscle movements to control contour feathers.

Feathers are durable, lightweight, and strong. No other animals have such complex structures growing from their skin.


# FEEDER CARE

There's more to attracting winter birds than just putting out seeds. Pitfalls can occur that will harm the birds you've attracted. For example, if you maintain a heated bird bath, never put glycerine in the water to keep it from freezing. This chemical will mat feathers, ending their insulating ability. Also, be sure to keep the bath water clean, since contamination from droppings can spread disease.

Sanitation in and around all winter feeders is a must. They should be cleaned frequently. Remove all droppings before feeders are refilled. Rake up any spilled seed or hulls from the ground around your feeder sites, especially if they are contaminated by droppings.

Shoveling fresh snow under a feeder will help. Tube feeders can be disinfected with a solution of five percent bleach in water, while a mild detergent and warm water will keep wooden feeders clean.

Sometimes even the best of intentions are foiled. My brother-in-law and his wife, who don't live in Madison, sent me this story that illustrates the need for care in feeding.

"One time, when we were visiting you, we stopped by Wild Birds Unlimited and bought 25 pounds of thistle seed for our pine siskins and other small birds. They really enjoyed it. I put the thistle seed in a plastic bucket and left it outside so that I could get to it. In the summer, we took down the feeder.

"Well, what with one thing or another, we forgot about the thistle seed and this fall I saw a bucket out by the pool and looked into it. The cover, being plastic, had weathered and broken. The seed was soaked and smelled terrible. I brought it into the house and commandeered some of Lois' pans and started to dry the stuff out in the oven. It smelled worse.

"I ended up spreading it on flat cardboard out in the garage. I placed an electric fan so that it would blow over the seed. Finally it dried out, and by leaving the garage door open, I got the odor out of there after three days. Then I filled the thistle feeder and lo! Birds wouldn't come near it. They wouldn't even land on the same branch that supported it.

"We now have a Wild Birds Unlimited here and I pointed out the problem with their thistle seed. They said it was probably moldy and no bird in its right mind would touch it, even if I had baked and blown it dry. So I threw away the results of my efforts, sanitized the bird feeder and got some more thistle seed.

"The back yard is now alive with little birds. My view of the whole thing is that they could have eaten the first seed, considering all the work I went to trying to save money — which I spent in gas and electricity trying to palatalize the gloppy stuff. But that is all over now. Lois will go out in the garage again and the neighbors no longer pass by with masks on their noses."

# TIGER OF THE TREE TOPS

Among the lesser known year-round residents of the Arboretum woods is the great horned owl, southern Wisconsin's largest owl. These birds are about two feet long, with feathers heavily barred in shades of brown, a white chin, and two prominent feather tufts on their heads, for which they are named.

Horned owls are active mostly at night and spend their days roosting in a leafy oak or densely needled pine tree. They sometimes can be spotted in early evening as they begin a night's hunt. The location of a day roost is sometimes given away by crows that gather in a noisy flock to harass the owl after it is discovered by a crow.

The owls' flight is strong and silent. They have acute hearing and sight, and can locate prey on the ground at surprising distances. Their voice consists of three or more deep, soft hoots ("hoo hoo-hoo") that have remarkable carrying power. Their calling is most often heard at night.

Great horned owls feed on many kinds of small mammals and birds. They take what is available for food; in our area primarily cottontail rabbits and mice. Their diet may also include domestic poultry and even house cats and small dogs. Except for the occasional owl that gets a poultry habit, they seem to do little long-term damage to their prey populations.

Horned owls become more audible in winter when their courtship period gets under way and they do much more calling. They are one of our earliest nesting species, laying their clutches of two to four eggs from late January into March.

Eggs are incubated from 26 to 30 days. The young are in the nest four to five weeks and then spend time in trees or on the ground until they can fly at about nine weeks of age. The young are tended by both parents all this time and for several weeks after they learn to fly.

Nests are made in old nests of red-tailed hawks, squirrels or crows; in hollow trees or on top of tree stubs. The owls do little nest building of their own. Usually they just clean out the debris of an old nest and add a few of their own feathers.

Horned owls are extremely protective of their nest sites and are perfectly willing and able to attack intruding humans. They can inflict serious wounds with their talons when they strike an unsuspecting trespasser.

In 1890, naturalist Ernest Thompson Seton wrote of great horned owls that, "Their untamable ferocity, their magnificent bearing, their carnivorous tastes, make me rank these winged tigers among the most pronounced and savage of the birds of prey." Whether his judgment is right or wrong, the great horned owl remains an awesome and desirable member of the Arboretum's natural community.


# WINTER FINCHES

Now that we're watching our cold-weather bird feeders, it's time to keep an eye out for winter finches. This group of small birds includes both residents of southern Wisconsin and wanderers from the north that don't migrate every year, but drift our way when their usual foods are in short supply.

There are nine species we might see. The residents include American goldfinch and house finch, while the visitors' list has pine siskin, purple finch, common redpoll, evening and pine grosbeaks, white-winged cross-bill and red crossbill.

The two crossbills and pine grosbeak are less apt to visit feeders than the others, but they may feed close by in the trees. The evening grosbeak is partial to box elder and ash seeds that remain on the trees, or leftover fruits of mountain ash and highbush cranberry. Crossbills favor the cones of pines, spruces and balsam fir. Their upper and lower bills are crossed, a good field mark and an adaptation for easily extracting seeds from cones.

Identification can be a problem. The bright yellow goldfinches of summer turn dull yellow and brownish olive in winter. They are not striped at any season. Pine siskins often hang out with goldfinches around feeders, but they are more gray-brown than yellow, although they have yellow patches on the rump and wings. Siskins always have heavily striped bodies.

The two grosbeaks are starling-sized and are easy to tell apart. Evening grosbeaks are stocky, with short tails, large white bills, yellow and olive brown bodies, and prominent white wing patches. Pine grosbeaks have long tails, black bills and mostly gray bodies. Plumages vary; males may have quite a bit of red on their head, throat and back. Females usually show some olive yellow.

Common redpolls are sparrow-sized and wear a red cap or "poll." Males also have rosy breasts. All are brown-striped on backs and undersides. The redpoll flocks that have come to my yard head straight for the white birch trees to pick seeds from the catkins.

The similarity of purple finches and house finches confuses many bird watchers. The males of both species have streaked brown backs with red on the head and chest, while their respective mates have no red and are heavily streaked above and below. Male purple finches are completely red across the top of the head, while a male house finch wears a brown cap. The house finch also has brown streaks on the belly which the purple finch lacks.

Female purple finches have a dark brown ear patch with a whitish eyebrow and cheek stripe. House finch females lack the distinct ear patch and eyebrow stripe. Both sexes of house finches are slimmer looking and less round-headed than their purple finch counterparts.

# COLD WEATHER HAWKS

Take a drive on the back roads of Dane County and watch for a large, dark hawk perched bolt upright on a fence post or small tree. If you see one, it is most likely to be one of our most impressive winter visitors, a rough-legged hawk (*Buteo lagopus*).

Roughlegs are characterized by mostly white tails with a broad black band at the tip, and are about the size of the more common red-tailed hawk. They come in two color phases. The light phase is the most common, with a brownish back, very dark belly, and a black patch on their underwings at the wrist. The dark phase is more spectacular, and also more rare, with nearly all its body in black, except for white in its underwings and tail. No other large hawk in Wisconsin has this color scheme.

Roughlegs are found in arctic regions, where they nest on cliffs or in tree tops. An occasional pair nests as far south as Wisconsin. Their winters are spent in the central United States and central Eurasia.

These are hawks of open country with a preference for marshes and open fields where they hunt their major food — mice and other small rodents. They also will feed on carrion. They often hover like a kestrel while they are hunting — a good characteristic to help you identify them.

Usually arriving in Wisconsin in early October, these birds remain with us as long as the ground is snow-free so they can hunt their food. They follow the snow line, staying south of it in winter and moving north from Wisconsin by the end of April. A prime, black-phase roughleg is one of my favorite winter birds.

## REDTAILS SOARING

Late February is a good time to start looking for pairs of red-tailed hawks soaring over Curtis Prairie or perched together at the top of a big oak on the edge of Gallistel Woods. Their togetherness is a sure sign that spring is near. Redtails begin their courtship in late February and March. It lasts about a month while nest-building and egg-laying are completed. Courting pairs spend much time soaring in great circles at high altitudes, often indulging in deep, looping aerial dives.

Redtails are among the largest Wisconsin hawks. Adults have a body length of about two feet and a wing span of 40 inches or more. They breed throughout the state, but are more common in the southern half. Some redtails are year-round residents in our southern counties. Others migrate to southern states. Still others move south just far enough to find areas where snow on the ground won't hinder their hunting.

Bird banders have determined that most of the redtails wintering in the state are adults. They are often seen perched on utility poles or in large trees in open areas. Their eyesight is excellent, and they can easily spot prey from their perches. They also hunt by slowly coursing across open fields and meadows.

Redtails feed primarily on small mammals such as mice, squirrels, chipmunks and rabbits. They occasionally take song-birds, snakes, earthworms, insects and domestic poultry. Several times I have seen them carry off the fresh carcasses of squirrels and cottontail rabbits killed by cars.

Adult redtails are easy to recognize, but first-year birds can be tricky. Adults have the distinctive unbanded rufous tail for which they are named. In addition, their undersides are faintly barred but quite pale, appearing nearly white in many individuals. Juveniles are much darker bodied with heavier barring on their breasts and dark, banded tails. They can be confused with other species such as red-shouldered hawks. Both age groups have the broad rounded wing shape and rounded tail characteristic of their species.

Life for redtails has not always been easy. In the early years of this century they were regularly killed by farmers and hunters because their predatory habits were perceived to be harmful to human interests.

In 1937, ornithologist A.C. Bent decried the indiscriminate slaughter of hawks and added that, "It will be a sad day indeed when we shall no longer see the great redtail sailing over the treetops on its broad expanse of wing and ruddy tail, or soaring upward in majestic circles until lost to sight in the ethereal blue, or a mere speck against the clouds."

While the writing may be overblown, the sentiment is not. Fortunately, stronger protective laws and more public understanding of how hawks live have not allowed Mr. Bent's fear to become fact.

## White On White — Weasels In Winter

As the landscape takes on quieter hues for the winter months, and humans don the warmer clothing they need, many members of the animal kingdom make corresponding changes — not only into heavier coats but also different colors.

While the non-breeding plumages of such birds as ducks and warblers are commonly noted, it seems to be less well-known that five species of Wisconsin mammals turn white in winter: White-tailed jackrabbit (Lepus townsendii), snowshoe hare (L. americanus), short-tailed weasel (Mustela erminea), long-tailed weasel (M. frenata), and least weasel (M. rixosa).

Of the five, the least and longtailed weasels have been found in the Arboretum, while the other three occur mostly west or north of Madison.

Least weasels are tiny, the smallest Wisconsin carnivores. They are six to eight inches long, including a one- to two-inch tail. They weigh a mere two ounces and have a body about as big around as your thumb. They are not common anywhere. Long-tailed weasels are about fifteen inches long, including a five-inch tail, and weigh six to nine ounces.

During the summer these animals are dark brown above with white undersides. Their molt to white pelage takes place in October and November, and summer pelage is usually complete by the end of March. Least and long-tailed weasels are completely white in winter, except that the long-tail retains a black tip on its tail. During the two annual molting periods, weasels have a mottled appearance. A few long-tails do not turn white at all, for reasons unknown.

Since weasels are active all winter, their white coats are important for protective coloration. Occasionally this camouflage is defeated; a snowless winter renders them quite conspicuous.

Least and long-tailed weasels feed primarily on mice, although the long-tail will kill other small mammals such as chipmunks, young cotton tail rabbits, ground squirrels and shrews. Birds of prey, in turn, are the weasel's enemies, although snakes, foxes and cats have been known to kill them as well. Both long-tails and short-tails are trapped for their winter pelts.

Mammalogist H.H.T. Jackson characterized the long-tail as "the most relentless, persistent, fearless and rapacious of carnivores in the pursuit of its prey." Other writers use adjectives such as pugnacious, energetic and curious. The least weasel's personality is like that of its long-tailed cousin, except on a smaller scale.

If you ever have a chance to watch a weasel in the wild, spend as much time observing as you can. Often the weasel is as interested in watching you as you are in watching the weasel. They are a joy to see.


# HOUSEHOLD WILDLIFE

Spring isn't far off, but winter is still here and perhaps another hike in the cold outdoors isn't what you're after. If so, an interesting project is to see what kinds of wildlife you can find in your house. There are lots of possibilities, depending on the age, size, design and neatness of the structure.

Among the smaller creatures you might identify are house spiders whose webs appear in corners of a room or on a protected window. If you have a damp basement, centipedes, millipedes, sow bugs (small, slate-colored crustaceans) and dormant mosquitoes may enjoy your hospitality.

A troublesome insect pest in storage areas is the silverfish, a flat, three-eighths-inch-long, silvery-white primitive species with a taste for book bindings, old paper, paste, glue and starch. Silverfish, along with clothes moths and cockroaches are year-round indoor residents.

Several other insects move into nooks and crannies around windows and in garages to hibernate. The flies that get into the house in fall are mostly adult female house flies. Cluster flies are similar to house flies, but heavier bodied and slower moving. They, too, hibernate in groups in corners of closets and other dark rooms.

Box-elder bugs are about a half-inch long with dark bodies and red stripes on their backs. They swarm in fall on porches and windows and like to hibernate inside warm buildings. If you don't have them at your house, the deck at the Arboretum's McKay Center is a great place to see them in large numbers come October. These bugs supposedly don't eat food or clothing but may damage house plants.

If you have firewood stored outside, be careful when you bring it inside. A cold log may house several types of beetles and other hibernating insects which may emerge if they are warmed up for several days. Remedy: burn the wood right away and don't store it indoors.

Mammals may be boarding with you, too. House mice and deer mice are partial to indoor living. House mice are solid dark gray in color, while deer mice are more brownish with white undersides. Both species have prominent ears.

Chipmunks have been known to spend the winter in woodpiles kept in attached garages. Flying squirrels sometimes invade attics. If it sounds like a track meet is going on above your bedroom ceiling some night, it could be a couple of flying squirrels on a nocturnal foray. Another attic resident in winter might be a little brown bat, but it's there only to hibernate.

Few homes in winter are without some form of wildlife.

# SOME BUGS LIKE THE SNOW

There aren't many insects out in the open during midwinter, but there is a small group collectively called "snow insects" which you might run across. Stone flies, crane flies, midges and springtails are in this category, although they differ widely in form and habits.

The springtails (*Achorutes*) we see in Wisconsin are perhaps the most abundant of the snow insects. They are dark in color and minute in size, so individuals are hard to see. However, on sunny days in February and March they often can be found in huge swarms on the surface of the snow at the base of a tree, or in footprints or wheel tracks.

One writer described a springtail swarm as "looking like a plate of mashed potatoes heavily sprinkled with black pepper." Even though they look like tiny specks, they can be extremely abundant, up to 10 million per acre according to one estimate.

If you find what looks like a dark smear on the snow, step closer and you may see that the smear is made of little specks, each of which is alive and leaping about. Springtails don't have wings, so they only crawl or jump.

They are exceptionally good at jumping. This is because they have a pair of extra legs attached to their rear ends. These legs are held forward and tight against their undersides with a clasping structure. When the clasp unhooks, the two legs push off against the snow (or ground) and the insect springs into the air. Obviously that's how they earned their name.

Springtails are commonly called "snow fleas," but there's no need to start scratching; they are not fleas. They don't get on dogs or people, don't suck blood and don't transmit disease. The details of their lives aren't well known. They just appear on the snow and start jumping as soon as the days get warmer.

Springtails have a diet of fungus filaments, moist dead plant tissues, insect droppings, spores, algae, bacteria, tree sap and microscopic animals. They're often found around maple trees when the trees are being tapped for sap.

# Illogical Ice

Did you ever wonder why ice floats? Logic seems to say that if heat rises and cold sinks, ice should form at the bottom of the pond and not at the top. However, water has a property that challenges our logic.

Here's how it works. As water cools, its density increases until its temperature drops to 39 Fahrenheit. From 39° to 32°, its density decreases. So at the freezing point (32°) a cubic foot of water weighs less than warmer water. Ice therefore forms at the surface.

Ice, being lighter than water, floats at the surface while the slightly warmer, heavier, unfrozen water stays beneath it. The ice may change in thickness as air temperatures change at its surface, but it still acts as insulation against freezing of the deeper waters.

Now that's cool!

# No Two Alike

There are many aspects of the outdoors that we take for granted, but which deserve a longer look.

What about snow? Some of us hate it and go south to escape it. Some of us grudgingly accept it and grumble while we shovel. And some of us admire its beauty and enjoy being out in it. Most of us don't know much about it beyond that it is cold, white and falls from the sky in winter, there is a lot more to it.

Snow falls as soft flakes formed when water vapor in the clouds is met by cold air and freezes into small ice crystals. Crystals then group together and become snowflakes.

All snowflakes are based on a hexagonal pattern, although their shapes vary widely. Most of them are six-sided, but some are twelve-sided and a few may be three-sided. The form of flakes depends entirely on conditions in the atmosphere. The most intricate shapes come from storms with the highest humidities. Conversely, storms with very low temperatures and humidity produce less complicated designs.

Snowflakes actually are colorless. It is the way their component crystals reflect light that makes them look white and reveals their shapes against a dark background.

Snowflakes have a mind-staggering characteristic: for all practical purposes no two flakes have exactly the same design. When you consider the billions of flakes that fall around the world, it would seem likely that by chance alone a flake pattern would repeat itself, but this does not seem to be the case.

This diversity of form was studied intensively for many years beginning in the late 1800s by W.A. Bentley, a life-long resident of Jericho, Vermont. Bentley spent his entire life studying snow. He developed a technique for photographing individual snowflakes under magnification. As snow was falling, he would catch individual flakes on a cold, dark metal plate and rush them to his camera in an unheated shed for photographing before the flakes melted. He took many thousands of snowflake pictures and never found any two exactly alike.

He became known as "Snowflake Bentley" and received worldwide recognition for his work. A fascinating book about his studies published in 1931 contains more than 2,000 photos of snowflakes, each different from the others. Bentley also photographed windowpane frost, sleet, dew, rime, clouds and mist.

Next time you go out in a snowfall, take along a hand lens, catch a snowflake on your sleeve, and discover the beauty of its structure. Then try to find another one just like it.


# THE MIDNIGHT LIGHT SHOW

Wisconsin has many spectacular sights in nature: gale-force winds on the Great Lakes, Canada geese feeding in a picked cornfield, a tall-grass prairie in full summer flower, and prairie chickens performing on their spring booming grounds are some examples. I'm sure everyone has other favorites.

One I find most impressive is the northern lights. Their scientific name is *Aurora borealis*. In our region, a good time to look for them is in the northern sky on a clear, calm and cold night in fall and winter.

Northern lights are usually greenish white, but sometimes show red or purple. The lights may come in several shapes — a steady glow, arcs, streaks, clouds or rays. The most spectacular form looks like waves of light rising into the sky only to disappear. Regardless of their form, these light shows cover a lot of space. They occur 60 to 600 miles above the earth and may be thousands of miles wide.

Northern lights are the result of an interaction between the earth's magnetic field and the sun. The sun ejects electrons and protons in what is called the "solar wind." Some of them reach the earth and are caught in its magnetic field. Eventually the electrons and protons are dumped on the upper atmosphere, where they strike the atoms and molecules of air, which in turn causes the energy that forms *Aurora borealis* to be released.

This complicated scenario took centuries to identify. Aristotle in the 4th century B.C. was one of the first to study northern lights. Detailed investigations by European scientists began in the 18th century.

For a long time the *Auroras* were thought to be associated with lightning, but modern studies disproved the lightning theory and identified the earth's magnetic field as their source.

Northern lights are most frequent when sunspots are most active. Sunspots are periodic violent eruptions of energy on the surface of the sun which can disrupt electronic communications for short periods on earth.

If your radio and television reception turns bad some winter night, it might be a good time to see if the northern lights are lit.

# GUIDE TO ARTISTS AND ILLUSTRATIONS

PATRICK SHEA has been illustrating articles for *NewsLeaf* since 1993. In addition, his drawings have been featured on Friends of the Arboretum note cards and displayed at the Arboretum's McKay Visitor Center. Outside of the Arboretum, his work has appeared in the international Birds in Art show, the teacher's guide for *Exploring Wisconsin Our Home,* and in *Airwaves,* Wisconsin Public Television's program guide. Patrick's work appears on the following pages:

ELISABETH DE BOOR began illustrating articles for *NewsLeaf* in 1995. Her drawings have also appeared on Friends of the Arboretum note cards and have been displayed at the McKay Visitor Center. She has studied sculpture and her etchings have been in exhibitions around the country. She has a degree in Fine Art and Graphic Design and recently served as a resident artist at the Edmund Niles Huyck Preserve and Biological Research Station in New York. Elisabeth's drawings appear on the following pages: